Other Hellboy books from Dark Horse Books

Hellboy:

Seed of Destruction (with John Byrne)
Wake The Devil
The Chained Coffin and Others
The Right Hand of Doom
Conqueror Worm
Strange Places
The Troll Witch and Others
Darkness Calls

Hellboy: Weird Tales Vol. 1
Hellboy: Weird Tales Vol. 2

Hellboy Junior

Hellboy: Odd Jobs
Hellboy: Odder Jobs

Hellboy: Emerald Hell

B.P.R.D.:

Hollow Earth & Other Stories
The Soul of Venice & Other Stories
Plague of Frogs
The Dead
The Black Flame
The Universal Machine
The Garden of Souls

The Art of Hellboy
The Hellboy Companion
Hellboy: The Art of the Movie
Hellboy II: The Art of the Movie

HELLBOY II
THE GOLDEN ARMY

A novel by
ROBERT GREENBERGER

Based on the motion picture screenplay by
GUILLERMO DEL TORO

Story by
**GUILLERMO DEL TORO &
MIKE MIGNOLA**

*Based on the
Dark Horse comic book created by*
MIKE MIGNOLA

DARK HORSE BOOKS®
Milwaukie

Hellboy II The Golden Army movie is a trademark and copyright of Universal Studios. Licensed by Universal Studios Licensing LLLP. All Rights Reserved.

Book design by Heidi Whitcomb and Amy Arendts
Cover photographs courtesy Universal Studios

Published by Dark Horse Books
A division of Dark Horse Comics
10956 SE Main Street
Milwaukie, OR 97222

darkhorse.com

First Dark Horse Books Edition: June 2008
ISBN 978-1-59307-954-3

Printed in U.S.A.

1 3 5 7 9 10 8 6 4 2

For Deb, who has stood by me through
all the craziness in the world.

But my thoughts are far off with Bethmoora in her loneliness, whose gates swing to and fro. To and fro they swing, and creak and creak in the wind, but no one hears them. They are of green copper, very lovely, but no one sees them now. The desert wind pours sand into their hinges, no watchman comes to ease them. No guard goes round Bethmoora's battlements, no enemy assails them. There are no lights in her houses, no footfall on her streets, she stands there dead and lonely beyond the Hills of Hap, and I would see Bethmoora once again, but dare not.

It is many a year, they tell me, since Bethmoora became desolate.

—Lord Dunsany

PROLOGUE

Douglas Army Base, NM
Christmas Eve, 1955

Snow in the form of fine flakes fell from the sky, landing in a thin coating atop the low-slung wooden barracks comprising Douglas Army base, a small post secreted away in the New Mexico desert. The few soldiers forced to endure the frigid cold, expected to reach the low twenties before midnight, were huddled in their parkas, weighted down by their rifles. They stood guard or patrolled, those moving etching patterns in the snow to mark their passage.

The base was built in a semicircle around a main headquarters; each of the two concentric circles was comprised of two small barracks buildings followed by a wide dirt road, followed by another set. Telephone poles and lampposts were the tallest objects in the camp.

Few knew what was going on in every building comprising the army base but they all remained unaware of the contents of one building that broke protocol and was marked A-51. Rumors, shared in the barracks during off-duty hours, speculated they were guarding the next stage in bomb making. After a nuclear bomb and hydrogen bomb, they wondered what could be even more destructive. Some theorized that it was not a warhead but instead some new rocket engine. After all, the flat desert had proven ideal for testing high-speed engines for jet planes. Many daydreamed while on patrol of being the test driver for some of those powerful vehicles, breaking the sound barrier like Chuck Yeager.

What made the building even more unusual was that it was the sole structure in the entire base to have a Christmas tree standing outside, nestled between the two sets of windows. It was decorated with outdoor lights and added the only exterior evidence that it was the holiday season.

The camp's complement heard odd noises coming from the building, and knew that it housed at least a few people although they only saw one—Trevor Bruttenholm, whom they presumed had been rescued from Europe during World War II. The assumption was that he was some sort of scientist and was housed to keep him from the Commies, since the Red Menace held the country in its imaginative grip. The best and the brightest had to be secured and Bruttenholm was just the only one at Douglas.

Not a single soldier could possibly imagine that the professorial-looking man was anything but a rocket scientist. In fact, these days he divided his time between his chosen profession and rearing a most unusual charge.

Bruttenholm, normally called Broom by most who knew him well, was blissfully unaware of the rumors that were associated with him and his work. He seemed unnaturally disinterested in such matters and concentrated instead on his chosen field. As America's leading authority in the paranormal, he focused instead on that which could not be seen or heard under normal conditions. His studies overseas brought him to the attention of Franklin Delano Roosevelt, who had seemingly created departments and bureaus dedicated to every facet of American life—save one. After listening to Broom discuss his work on decoding the Nazis' encryption systems, their talk turned to Hitler's fascination with the occult. Roosevelt was not one to go for such unconventional thoughts, considering himself too worldly for that sort of thing. However, he recognized that Hitler was far from alone in his beliefs and there were most certainly things that rational science could not yet explain.

It was during the Second World War that the president signed an executive order that created the Bureau of Paranormal Research and Defense, hiding its operating budget to avoid ridicule. Broom was its leader and that is how he wound up in Scotland in 1944, witness to the miraculous arrival of a child on a cold evening, not unlike the event being celebrated that very night.

He was there to stop Grigori Yefimovich Rasputin from bringing the Ogdru Jahad, the Seven Gods of Chaos, through a portal that was opened by mixing science with sorcery. While the wily Russian managed to open the gateway to another realm, the U.S. Army did stop him but not before something came through. While not one of the dreaded gods, it was also not human. Rasputin said it was *Anung Un Rama* but what the soldiers found was a tiny, bright-red-skinned, horned baby, complete with tail and an oversized gauntlet of a right hand that seemed to be made of stone.

Looking across their small, spartan living quarters, Broom saw his charge sitting contentedly watching television. His mind flashed back to the first time he saw Hellboy, a small, scared creature ripped from his home and brought to the cold hills of Scotland. That nickname the soldiers gave the infant seemed right from the first time they spoke it. They bonded over a Baby Ruth bar and the young demonlike being allowed himself to be cared for by this tall, gaunt man.

Broom remained rail thin despite the intervening eleven years. His adopted son, though, had grown. From careful measurements, which Hellboy endured several times a year, the researcher concluded that the boy was aging far slower than humans. So, even though it was eleven years for him, the demon-born youth appeared and acted far younger. The very first signs of adolescence seemed to be upon him as his horns were gaining sharper points and he seemed ready for a growth spurt.

He had long ago given up on the baby-expert books he initially bought, finding more to fear from Dr. Spock than his charge. Broom was mentally composing an entirely new book on rearing a demon in a human world and he took his cues more from tomes of folklore from around the globe than from medical texts. Mixed in with his books on demonology and the paranormal, there were collections from Europe, Asia, the South Pacific, and most recently some newly unearthed original volumes from Ireland. The stories provided him tips on handling the boy, but they also gave him more interesting things to read to Hellboy than the standard pap that passed for children's literature.

These days his chief competition for the boy's attention was the black-and-white television the army had installed only a year before. It helped occupy the active youth since he was largely confined to their barracks. To the adult, the children's offerings on television were hardly any better than the age-appropriate books, but at least they were able to find the occasional program they could both enjoy.

But not *that*.

He glanced once more at the boy, enraptured by what appeared to be a cow singing on the screen. Something about it bothered Broom, so he chose to ignore it rather than engage in a fight with the boy. No, today was a day for peace and harmony, even if only one of them really celebrated the holiday. Broom busied himself with adding the last ornaments to their modest Christmas tree, in its wooden stand near the corner. The pickings were slim, out here in the desert, but Broom used his contacts in Washington to secure trees for the entire base, figuring the gesture of goodwill would not be lost on the bored soldiers. To date, only their outdoor tree was decorated and lit, a concession from the camp commander who didn't go in for ostentatious displays even for Christmas.

The ornaments he used came from here and there; no real family heirlooms survived his travels. Instead, there was a generic nutcracker from the ballet, a few reindeer, a smiling jolly Santa Claus and some ceramic snowflakes. With a practiced eye, Broom placed the final ornament on a lonely branch toward the top and then stood up. He stretched, working out the kinks in his back, noting the coming of middle age. His work had the habit of being done in the dark, bent over desks or caskets and as it was, physically, he appeared older than he was, with his pale, olive skin and thinning hair.

His chore done, he closed up the ornament box, intending to replace it in the closet. Instead, his eye was drawn to a trail of candy wrappers between the tree and the couch where Hellboy sat mesmerized. Broom had offered to let him decorate the tree, but the activity didn't engage him this year as the adult had hoped. Another sign of coming puberty, he supposed. Hellboy placed a few ornaments, grew bored and asked to watch television.

He stooped down and collected several wrappers, their crinkle competing with the television to fill their living quarters with sound.

"Son . . . would you please turn off that dreadful puppet and brush your teeth," Broom finally said, tiring of the antics on the screen.

"Howdy Doody."

"I beg your pardon?" Broom could hardly make out the words what with the boy chewing noisily on yet another Baby Ruth. Given that his first human food was something sweet, it was quite the struggle through the years to introduce more nutritious fare to his diet. In time, Broom realized Hellboy metabolized food differently and his body's needs were not at all in sync with other children. As a result, Broom came to accept that the candy and snack chips Hellboy seemed to prefer had no deleterious effects on his growth. Not that he stopped trying to get him to eat a balanced diet since, sooner or later, Hellboy was going to be studying or working with humans and he needed to know what was expected in polite company.

"He's not a puppet. Howdy Doody is real. He talks," the boy said, his current candy bar now finished. A chubby choc-olate-smudged finger pointed at the screen, filled with the image of the wooden puppet the children's program was named for. Broom could not understand the allure and never bothered to learn the names of the characters of this, Hellboy's favorite show. Normally it ran during the afternoon, but being Christmas Eve, it ran later which interrupted their routine.

"Well, Mr. 'Dee-dee-doo-doo' has to say 'good night,'" Broom announced. He walked to the television and turned it off, the picture collapsing in on itself like a black hole until the only light remained a dot in the center of the screen.

"Remember, you have to be asleep when *he* comes down this chimney," Broom said, now closer to the couch. Hellboy looked up, annoyed at his show being over early and at what he was being told.

"It's not even a chimney, Pops," he complained, a whine in his voice. Hellboy looked around their living quarters, as if a chimney might have miraculously been built when he wasn't looking. Seeing none, his shoulders sagged and his tail drooped.

"My son," Broom began but was cut off.

"How will he fit through it?" the boy asked, fully engaged on the topic.

In his most conspiratorial voice, Broom replied, "*He* has his ways." With a grand gesture, he pointed toward the black open pipe stove that was aglow with reddish embers. Its heat made the room comfortable, almost stuffy, and Broom fought off an urge to yawn.

Dissatisfied with the answer, the boy crossed his arms and seemed to set himself in place. "I want to wait up! Watch him do it!"

"Nonsense," Broom countered. "Who ever heard of waiting up for Santa Claus?" At least, in this way, Hellboy was exactly like every other child on each continent. That thought brought him comfort since so often his mind fretted over just how easily his charge would adapt to the world.

Hellboy seemed to think about how long to prolong a fight he knew he could not win. Instead, he decided to get something in exchange for his acquiescence. "Okay," he began in a happier tone. "I want a story, then."

Shaking his head slowly from side to side, Broom answered, "No, no, no. No stories tonight."

This was an argument they went through more than once and each knew his part. Now it was Hellboy's turn to try a new bargain.

"Just one," he said brightly. "And then I'll go to bed, right away."

Broom stared at him expectantly.

"And I'll brush my teeth! I promise."

Looking down at the boy, Broom's stern expression melted into a smile. Bargain sealed.

Even though there was the promise of a story, Hellboy dawdled at getting ready. There were toys to put away, a stocking to be hung near the stove. Broom directed and cajoled while considering which tale to tell. He had decided on something new, something to get the boy's mind off the impending arrival of Santa. As Hellboy put on white pajamas covered with cowboys, Broom studied a shelf of books and selected one of the new Irish volumes. It was old, bound in leather which had cracked in places from age and use. Oversized compared with the others, it was filled with colorful woodcut images and large writing with ornate script and designs in the margins. He doubted there were many copies of this particular book left in circulation and considered himself quite fortunate to have found it while seeking other books in his unending research.

Finally, Hellboy appeared at his side by the stove. He took a seat and Broom showed him the cover and settled back in his own chair. With a flourish, Broom opened the book and began to read.

"'It is said that at the dawn of time . . . Man, Beast, and all Magical Beings lived together under Aiglin, the Father Tree . . . '"

Hellboy moved closer to Broom, angling the chair so he could see the pages better even though he could not yet read all the words. The picture fascinated him while the script seemed overly fussy. The Father Tree was huge, stately, and broad, with many limbs and leaves. Under it, in silhouette only, were a multitude of creatures the nature of which could only be guessed at. Hellboy thought he was pretty good at guessing and filling in the details, so the orcs and goblins took shape and grew far more colorful.

The youthful demon moved closer, clutching his black cat Clump, who didn't like being squeezed. He pointed at a large mechanical silhouette, different and more menacing than the other images on the colorful page. "What's that—?"

"Child," Broom said softly, closing the book. "If you're going to interrupt . . ."

Quickly, Hellboy and Clump sat back down, the chair inching even closer to Broom and the book. "No-no. We're listening," he insisted.

Broom nodded with approval. "Very good, then." He continued to read from the beginning:

"'It is said that at the dawn of time . . . Man, Beast, and all Magical Beings lived together under Aiglin, the Father Tree.

"'But Man had been created with a hole in his heart. A hole that no possession, power, or knowledge could fill . . . And in his infinite greed, Man dreamt of expanding his dominion over the entire earth.'"

Hellboy was absently petting Clump, who purred in his lap, his focus intent on the book and its pictures. Each picture was like a frozen television screen and was a starting point, allowing him to make up images to fill in the gaps. Orcs, goblins, elves, fairies, and dragons all became distinct from one another, and he actually felt a chill as he conjured up an image of a dragon, drool dripping from one exposed fang and hitting the ground with a sizzle.

"'And so it came to pass that a bitter war began between the Magical Beings—the Sons of the Earth and the Sons of Adam.'"

In his mind's eye, Hellboy watched as sparkles of colorful magic flew across the land, striking down wave after wave of sweaty, bearded men. The creatures of the Earth, those who could fly, weave magic, breathe fire, and more, went up against the helmeted, armored men who required weapons such as shields and swords to even the odds. Lances stuck deep into the thighs of Orcs, who merely swatted them away and then clubbed the humans. A fairy fell from an arrow, the archer laughing at his good fortune. The air was filled with metal striking bone, leather ripping, and wooden shields shattering from blows that whistled as they struck. A fire broke out from a dragon's blast and the aroma of burning, charred wood and flesh now filled the area. Hellboy swallowed, avoiding gagging on the imaginary plume of darkening smoke.

What the humans lacked in inherent ability was seemingly made up for with sheer numbers and an unprecedented fierceness. The battles were long, hard, and bloody. Wings were sheared off, arms were lost, families torn asunder. Time dropped away, and the war continued unabated.

" 'The blood of many an Elf, Ogre, and Goblin was spilled.

" 'And their sovereign: King Balor, the one-armed king of Elfland, watched the slaughter in dread and despair.' "

Hellboy imagined the king, a noble figure, his hair an iron gray, his eyes blazing with determination. His golden crown affixed atop his head, his ermine cloak flowing behind him as he paced back and forth in his stone castle, a figure of despair.

" 'But one day, the Master of the Goblin Blacksmiths entered the courtyard and offered to build the King a new, mechanical army. Seventy times seventy soldiers that would never know hunger or pain and could not be stopped.' "

"How many is that?" Hellboy asked, breaking his silence.

Broom paused briefly to do the math and said, "Imagine nearly five thousand fresh soldiers which could turn the tide for either side."

" 'Prince Nuada, Silverlance, son of Balor, full of pride and anger, begged his Father to agree—for this army would surely hand them victory—would it not?' "

Silverlance. Hellboy liked the name and the image it conjured forth of a younger man, resembling his father in profile, with glistening black hair, and where the king was bedecked in gold, the son was similarly clad in silver. While the father fretted, Nuada was trembling for action. Hellboy wasn't so sure he liked the impatient prince.

"'And the King, who loved his son too much, agreed: *Build me this army,* he said . . .

"'So, the Goblins worked night and day and day and night in their fiery workshops—BIM-BAM-BIM-BAM—until the pale winter moon was high in the sky . . .'"

The boy sat there, Clump still in his lap, oblivious to the wild thoughts racing through his owner's mind. Hellboy saw the sun glinting off an endless supply of tireless soldiers, tall and broad. Each was identically dressed in a fanciful uniform, figures of perfection.

"'A magical crown was forged that would allow those of Blood Royal to command the new army.'"

Hellboy studied the crown as drawn, twisting metal in a simple circle, with markings in a language he couldn't possibly understand. What it lacked in majesty it made up for in power.

"'*I am King Balor, leader of the Golden Army. Is there anyone who disputes my right?* And in his throne room and across the world, no one uttered a word . . .

"'And so the army swore fealty to him . . .'"

Hellboy finally tore his gaze from the book and looked up at his adoptive father. He couldn't imagine why Broom had grown so much older so fast in the last decade, but the man was looking more weathered, the beginnings of gray, like Balor, seen in his hair. Broom noticed the look and paused in his reading.

"But wait," Hellboy said, interrupting. "What if someone had challenged him?"

Broom frowned at the question. He glanced at the book to see if he missed something then looked at the boy. Clump looked up as well.

"But no one did," he replied. "No one of royal blood."

"But what would've happened? Would they have a fight—to control the army monsters?"

He anticipated a stern word from Broom, who disliked questions during story time. Today, though, he seemed more thoughtful. Maybe he was new to the story as well, and didn't have all the answers. Hellboy knew Broom spent his days seeking answers to questions, the kind, the man told him more than once, that most men dare never ask. Hellboy always wondered why people would be afraid to ask questions and swore to himself he'd never be afraid to ask.

"Most likely a challenge must be answered." Broom thought a bit more then his face shifted into one the boy knew all too well. "You want to hear the rest of the story or not?"

"Yes . . . please." Time to stop asking questions. Besides, he was also a little sleepy and wanted to ensure he heard the ending.

Broom continued to read as he turned the page. "'So the world was changed and the next time the Sons of Adam marched, they felt the earth tremble beneath their feet and saw the sky darken with monstrous shapes.'"

Hellboy looked at the colorful picture of men, a more ragged assemblage than the perfect rows of the Golden Army. They were dirty and angry, clutching their spears, lances, shields, and swords. This was to be the final battle, he thought. It was a cloudy, gray day, to match the army's mood.

"'The Golden Army knew no bounds, had no remorse, felt no loyalty. It knew not the difference between man, woman, or child. It extinguished all human life without pause or remorse.'"

The next picture showed the carnage's aftermath. Hellboy tried to imagine the battle but all he could conjure were fleeting images of swinging weapons and falling humans. Women and children were mixed in suddenly and he grew sad at the notion of so much innocent life being lost. It was not something he wanted to dwell on, he decided.

"'And King Balor's heart grew heavy, for this victory was gained at too high a price.'"

The next picture, filling only a quarter of the page, showed King Balor bent over his throne, his arm behind his back. Shadows seemed to be crowding him and he looked anything but the victor of the conflict.

"'He called a truce and divided the crown into three pieces: one for the Sons of Adam and two for the Sons of the Earth. In exchange, Man would keep to the cities and the Sons of the Earth would own the forests. This truce, he proclaimed, would be honored by their sons and the sons of their sons until the end of time.'"

In his throne room, the picture showed Hellboy how the king handed a piece of the crown to a man in his finest garb. The man, with shaggy hair and a well-trimmed beard, accepted the fractional crown in his right hand, his left resting on the pommel of his sword. Beside the man was Nuada, looking none too happy with the exchange, his own hand wrapped around his wide belt, next to his dagger. Before the boy could wonder why, Broom kept reading.

"'But Prince Nuada did not believe in the promises of Man. And it is said that he went into exile, vowing to return on the day the Sons of the Earth most needed him.'" The book showed Nuada walking away from his father and the court, heading toward the setting sun in the distance, the land before him devastated from the terrible war that had recently concluded.

"'And the Golden Army lay dormant, locked inside the earth waiting.'"

There was an image of a vast chamber, filled with the ranks of golden soldiers, standing at attention and poised to receive new orders, their armor reflecting in the ten thousand torches used by the goblins that locked them away. The notion that they had nothing to do troubled Hellboy but he was even more disturbed at the notion that the king allowed them to remain intact. If they were that terrible to humans, what if they were used against the king's people? The thought was too horrible to imagine so the boy hugged Clump, who chose that moment to leap free and go prowl the barracks. Hellboy was left alone and unhappy about it.

Unsettled, he got up and wandered toward the bathroom. Absently, he grabbed his toothbrush, added a dab of toothpaste and began to scrub. The bathroom was like the rest of the base, clean and drab in appearance, functional without any sense of comfort.

Broom also seemed concerned over what he was reading, so much so that he paused a moment and then followed the boy into the bathroom and continued. "'. . . and there it is to this day. Awaiting the day the crown is made whole again. Silent, still, and indestructible.'"

Hellboy rinsed then asked, "What does it mean 'industrable'?"

"Indestructible," Broom corrected him, closing the book softly. "It means: no one can destroy them." His hand rested against the leather cover and his eyes seemed far away.

"So—no one can do anything to them," Hellboy began. Now he knew why King Balor did nothing. He couldn't.

"No one."

"Not even you?!" He heard the unsteadiness of his own high-pitched voice.

The question seemed to catch Broom by surprise and he hesitated responding. Hellboy was also confused why the question would cause him to smile, ever so slightly. "No—not even I. Now go to sleep, my child."

Scooping up Clump, Hellboy made his way across the room to his bed. With a little hop, he landed softly atop the covers and then reached to the wall. A crimson hand grasped a shining cap pistol, its faux pearl handle dwarfed in his palm. Ready to ward off any danger, Hellboy scrambled under the covers, thoughts of Santa Claus gone from his mind.

"But it's just a story, right, Pops?" He looked imploringly at Broom, who hovered over the bed, shadows playing across his face, his expression unreadable.

"Is it, now?"

That was just unfair, to leave the question unanswered. Hellboy was not at all ready to accept the story as a legend. He burrowed under the covers, his head barely peeking out from the top.

"Yeah, c'mon—those guys—they can't be real."

Broom nodded gravely at the boy and smiled, not at all convincingly. "Well, my son," he said, "I'm sure you'll find out."

Hellboy raised his head from the sheets and blankets, his gun still firmly in his grasp, and smiled at his father. The idea of actually learning the truth sounded so exciting.

With visions of golden soldiers and not sugar plums dancing in his head, the boy drifted off to sleep and Broom walked back to the bookcase and gently shelved the volume.

CHAPTER ONE

Rain fell steadily outside, running into storm drains and funneled into New York City's sewer system. The system, largely built in the nineteenth century and haphazardly maintained ever since, had cracks along fittings and joints, allowing waste water to run freely down the tunnel walls, staining the concrete and tile work. Mildew and algae of varying sorts discolored the imagery, be it graffiti or signage. A brownish stain streaked a most impressive decoration, one the city's fathers had never approved of adding when the pipes had been laid and bedrock tunneled out decades earlier.

The image was a huge tree, stylized beyond your typical genealogical family history, its branches heavy with runes and names in a language long thought dead. On either side of the tree were carvings of events thought fable, moments of history preserved with loving detail. Ogres, fairies, and trolls were depicted in varying activities, the children of the earth in their natural habitat. That such an ancient relic was preserved in a sewer tunnel proved how far the Sons of Adam's domination of the planet had grown.

A shadow was cast against the scene of a troll at play. The figure moved with grace, each movement a sign of practice, exuding strength. The arms slashed through the air, extending a broadsword against an imaginary foe. Each parry and thrust resounded with a faint echo in the tunnel, fighting with the persistent sound of dripping water. Each footfall splashed water high into the air, adding to the sounds of activity.

A sole man trained in the tunnel, his only witnesses the images on the walls, who all owed him fealty. His breathing was heavy but controlled, his training session well into its second hour. Sweat ran down his pale bare-chested form, flying from his body as he twisted and moved, each drop joining the rainwater at his feet. His leather boots and silken pants each made different sounds in the dank tunnel. An occasional grunt accompanied thrusts and as he wound down his practice, he exerted his will and the sword began to shimmer, the metal elongated until the sword became a lance.

With the mid-range weapon, he now swiped at the air, swinging its sharp end up until it nearly scraped the tunnel's top. He swung it in a complete circle around his body one way, then another. After several more minutes, he ended his session with a vicious thrust that would have torn an opponent in two.

But there were no opponents. And there was but one companion, well-versed in the imagined carnage such a weapon could wreak. The silent, still figure watched; his heavy-lidded eyes the only things moving in time with the lance.

The man lowered the weapon and leaned it against the wall. With two steps, he was beside two large iron boxes, each ornate in decoration.

"Our little friends," the voice began. It was a hard voice, its steeliness overcoming any sense of warmth found in the words. "Bought them today . . . haven't fed them."

The figure reached for the rest of his clothes, a matching

silken and embroidered shirt and robes. As he put them on his still-cooling body, the man continued. "I'll go up first. You'll follow." He adjusted the robe so it sat straight across his shoulders.

The bulky figure nodded in understanding.

At his feet, the two boxes shook, vibrating against the concrete, causing ripples in the fetid water. In the silence of the tunnel, harsh, angry sounds could be heard coming from within the metallic containers.

The man smiled, bent down, and picked up one of the two boxes. He stepped through a gaping hole in the concrete, leaving his chamber and entering a new tunnel. On the other side, a subway headed downtown rattled, causing more water to shake loose, splashing everywhere. As he moved into the gap, he looked just once over his shoulder at his silent, hulking companion.

"And remember, Wink: *Don't be shy.*"

With that, the man effortlessly leapt into the air, fingers reaching out for the side of a wall. Fingertips found purchase in the uneven brickwork with toes quickly following, scraping against the slick surface. Undaunted, he quickly crawled up the façade and reached a ledge. Gaining a toehold, he swiveled and rested his back against the corner and turned his attention across the street.

Selecting his next target, powerful legs propelled him through the air, the rain ignored, and he landed with ease on a building diagonally across the street, his movement undetected by the passing traffic below. Like a spider, he crawled further up the new building, reaching heights that would have seemed impossible for any biped to achieve.

Below, his silent, inhuman comrade watched, waiting for a signal to join his master.

———

Manhattan
September 26
8:00 P.M.

Nestled amidst the glass and steel structures that made up midtown Manhattan was Blackwood's Auction House. While not the largest or even the most architecturally impressive of the city's offerings, that night the four-story building was the center of attention. Despite the rain, which continued to lightly fall, the block was ablaze with beams slicing through the darkness, generated from giant truck-mounted klieg lights.

At the building's entrance, limousine after limousine slowly rolled forward and took its turn emitting its passengers. Then, the black stretch vehicles moved out of sight, vanishing into the misty night air, all eyes focused on the people walking inside the building.

This was to be no ordinary auction as promised by the huge sign affixed above the glass-and-chrome doorway: TREASURES OF PRE-CHRISTIAN EUROPE. Nothing would go cheap and the very promise of owning something prestigious brought out the elite. Reporters milled on the periphery, noting which bluebloods and minor celebrities were in attendance. There were CEOs, foundation chairs, university presidents, actors, and Old Money mixing where normally they kept to their own worlds. Tonight, though, the lure of owning a piece of their collective past was too strong and they arrived, ready to spend.

The actual auction room was packed, as everyone politely took their seats. Each row was five seats across, with a wide aisle separating them, bisecting the room in two. All were resting comfortably in their finery, numbered paddles lying in their laps, waiting to be used. At the far left side of the room was a long banquet table, covered in a dark maroon tablecloth. A team of men and women manned the phones, taking bids from those unable—or unwilling—to attend in person. As a result, a constant murmur was heard from that corner, the only sound beyond the authoritative tones of the auctioneer.

Time slipped by without notice as lot after lot was paraded out once more and examined by those who missed visiting the showroom or couldn't be bothered to flip through the lavish catalog. Money was spent without hesitation as bits and pieces of the past were purchased by new owners, who no doubt intended to display them for prestige rather than any real fascination with history.

People came and went, some to claim their property, others to arrange loans so they could compete for future lots. The doors silently swung open and closed repeatedly since the actual selling began.

Now, an older woman—her skin taut from repeated nips and tucks, her hair sprayed into shape, now hard as a helmet—entered. Her gown was a one-of-a-kind Italian number in golden hues with matching dyed heels. The makeup was expertly applied and no doubt the entire ensemble cost more than the auctioneer was paid for the evening and that was before adding on what the jewelry on her ears, fingers, and neck could be appraised for. In her arms was a Pomeranian that sniffed the air but was motionless otherwise. The dog was equally groomed and quaffed, complete with matching jeweled necklace. While Blackwood's normally frowned on pets, this woman was a repeat customer and her annual account more than called for an exception.

Three steps behind her, clearly knowing his place, was an even older man, less well groomed despite the immaculate tuxedo. He was thin and somewhat stooped, preventing the designer outfit from properly fitting his frame despite expert tailoring. His slicked-back hair was thinning and was in danger of being long enough to be considered a comb over, but few paid him attention, considering how his wife ensured she was the focus of their attention.

"Next lot, number 776," the auctioneer called in a smooth, professional voice. Despite not being loud, it carried through the room thanks to a discreet microphone before him. A woman in a red gown, that hugged her well and commanded attention from the audience, walked onto the stage carrying the item just announced, a dusky stone statue with bloated features. Television monitors artfully spaced around the room brought the towering object into focus, carefully avoiding the woman's ample cleavage. Heads craned to examine the item, others retained their focus on the woman, not at all caring to own something so . . . vulgar.

"An important votive figure—a fertility goddess—dating approximately to 15,000 to 10,000 BCE. Found in a loess deposit in a terrace about thirty meters above the Shannon River. We'll open the bidding at $300,000."

Tuxedoed stewards discreetly held small cameras and focused on those who stirred, seeking the first paddle to be raised. They were practiced at spotting body language that showed who was ready to pounce and who was not at all interested.

Away from the auction room, stewards crisscrossed the hallways, pushing carts containing future auction items, each awaiting their brief turn in the spotlight. One man in a dark suit, his brown hair casually brushed to the side, walked down one hall en route to collecting one of the precious items.

Passing a window, he saw a breeze playing with the white curtains, letting in both a chill and some of the rain, causing the carpet to grow dark from dampness. He walked past the window, noting its condition, but kept going until he stopped to process the information, realizing it was bad to let in both

the draft and the rain. After all, the polished wood frame
might warp if too damp and given that they were floor-to-
ceiling windows that would be a problem. The man put aside
his thoughts of his objective and returned to the window,
pausing to glance outside to momentarily admire the view.
He looked directly across the street, hoping for a glimpse of
something provocative, but all the windows were dark, keeping their contents a secret.

The steward then looked below, seeing the rain form
puddles here and there and the sharp points of the spiked
fence surrounding the auction house's perimeter. As he concentrated on the street, a smattering of gravel fell on his
shoulder. At first he brushed it away, absently thinking nothing
of it until he realized he was so far up, nothing should have
caused debris to fall. The rain certainly wasn't coming down
that hard.

Craning his neck, he leaned a little further out the window
to examine the floor above him. The fact that a man was
miraculously affixed to the wall caused several things to happen at once. The steward's eyes went wide, his jaw dropped,
and his heart began to race. Words began to form in his
throat, either questioning the intruder or calling for help—
he'd never know because in that moment, the figure in the
sodden robes reached down and yanked. Suddenly, the steward found himself leaving his feet and then exiting the building. A powerful grip ruined the creases of his now-wet suit
jacket and was all that held him in place, dangling a lethal
distance over the street.

The other hand, sinewy and calloused, clamped over his
mouth, ensuring sounds would never emerge.

In the distance, heard over a speaker broadcasting the auction
for those not in the room, the steward heard the voice
continuing.

"Three hundred seventy-five, and . . . we have four hundred.
"And four hundred fifty thousand dollars.
"Going once, going twice. Sold."

The strange, pale man, still and regal in his bearing despite hanging almost upside down from the building's exterior, heard the crack of a gavel. He then turned his gaze on the steward who struggled but made no sound.

"A silent human," the man said in a voice that was rough and full of disdain. The steward felt something tingle on his face and thought he was on the verge of a panic attack but then the hand clamping his jaw was released. The tingle stopped and he tried to open his mouth and found he could not. His tongue beat against a solid wall of skin and he sharply inhaled through his nose since, suddenly, his mouth appeared to have vanished.

"Almost as good as a dead human."

The man held up his right hand and the steward silently cried out—for there, in his palm, were lips and even teeth. His lips, still moving, and his teeth stained from too much caffeine. It was some bizarre magic trick, he determined. Some sort of hypnosis had to have been employed because body parts didn't just transfer from one person to another.

Then, the hand seemed to wave in farewell and the steward felt the hand grasping his jacket slacken. He began to fall backward, knowing for certain that gravity was about to gain control of his body and that was not going to end well.

No longer was he held by the man who stole his mouth, whose expression was cold and unfeeling. Instead, he was getting wet from the rain, ruining his suit, and the wind began to whip past him as he accelerated. Just then he remembered the spiked fence and knew this would hurt.

He wanted to scream, to let the world mark his passing. But he had no mouth and though he must scream, he could not.

Watching from above, the intruder seemed satisfied that his aim was true and the blood welling through the man's punctured chest and leg made him briefly smile. Then, turning his attention to the window, he crawled closer and then acrobatically flipped himself through the open window, landing on the balls of his feet, without making a sound.

"And now, for our next item. Lot number 777."

He listened intently as he brushed off droplets and wall debris. Taking another moment to straighten out his robes, smoothing the silk so as to be presentable when he made his entrance.

"For the first time at auction. A piece of the royal crown of Bethmoora . . . Early first century . . ."

Two stewards entered the room, wheeling an oaken box. With great ceremony, they opened it and withdrew a maroon velvet pillow. Nestled atop it was a semicircle in gold, ornately decorated. This was clearly an item of some worth and importance. People straightened up to peer past those in front to see it live, not on a camera. Even the woman's dog seemed to look at it.

At that moment, the doors opened and the man in silken robes and leather boots entered. His dark, ornately designed garb, compared with the formal attire of the other men, immediately caused a stir. Everyone turned to see who entered and then couldn't take their eyes off him. His pale, white skin, long white hair and handsome features were arresting. Murmurs began as people noted the sharp tip atop each ear. His eyes were rimmed in dark shadows but were red and his lips were black. A fine line ran across his cheeks, over the bridge of his nose and seemed more birthmark than tattoo. They all tried to identify him as maybe an Internet mogul, a Saudi prince, or a South American athlete.

"Please, please—ladies and gentlemen . . . may I have your attention," the auctioneer called, actually raising his voice to command their interest.

It took a few moments for the people to turn, most in response to the passing figure as he strode down the wide aisle between the seats and approached the podium. As he neared, the room's lights flickered and then blinked off. A second later, just as people began to exclaim in surprise, emergency lights came to life. The room was now cast in shadows which seemed to make the man appear larger and more formidable.

The auctioneer cleared his throat and asserted his authority by trying to go forward, maintaining decorum and hopefully control.

"As I was saying . . . exquisite Celtic workmanship from a long-lost culture . . ."

He was cut off by the pale man whose words echoed louder than his, even without a microphone.

"Lost? Not at all. Oh, no. Forgotten by you perhaps, but very much alive."

Murmurs began once more and stewards scrambled toward the doors, ready to block the exits or assist people in leaving. No one was certain what was happening and that paralyzed them.

"Sir," the auctioneer began, once more trying to be in command. "Sir. Would you please identify yourself?"

The man straightened his shoulders and stood his ground a dozen feet from the front of the room. All eyes were riveted on him and he basked in it for the briefest of moments.

"I am Prince Nuada, Silverlance, Son of King Balor, and I am here to reclaim what is rightfully mine."

With that, he continued forward and helped himself to the golden arc. The stewards nearest him remained transfixed. The auctioneer, though, was not, maybe given his distance from the mysterious, threatening figure. He grabbed a phone located within the base of his podium and spoke hurriedly to the steward nearest him.

"Security! Call Security . . ."

Before a steward could carry out the order or the auctioneer himself could make a connection, there was a horrible sound just outside the room. Wood and metal bending and breaking made separate noises but here they formed a horrid duet as the main doors burst open, splinters flying into the room, causing those nearest the door to duck. Human screams followed the ending echo of the destroyed doors.

What caused the doors to obliterate were two uniformed security guards, who gracelessly flew through the air and landed in the aisle. This caused even more of the audience to scream and move out of the way. Things seemed to be happening quickly and no one seemed to know what to do. The auctioneer presumed the intruder was behind everything that was turning the biggest night of his life into a nightmare. He craned his neck to see the two men lying in a heap, noting the blood on one and the odd angle of the other's right arm.

What amazed him the most, though, was the hand sans arm that seemed to deposit the men on the floor, then hang in the air for a moment. The oversized mitt then retreated, seemingly floating backward toward the hall. In the doorway, though, it reconnected to the arm of a very large, very broad, hairless and most definitely inhuman being. The heavily muscled arms and legs were mostly bare, the ankles and feet wrapped in what might have been animal skin or leather or some horrible combination of both. A loincloth and broad belt circled his waist and above it, covering his stomach and most of his chest, were straps of leather in a crisscross pattern. The hands and wrists were covered in studded gloves. His head was oval with what appeared to be tusks jutting down from his jaw, ending in blunt points and likely made of bone. The tip of the right tusk was missing, leaving a rough edge. His sparse hair was coarse and flowed high from the midpoint of his skull all the way down his back, framing his face, with an unruly tuft between the tusks. The blunt nose was a mere ridge with nostrils set high by the eyes, which were glowing and pupil-less, making him even more frightening in appearance. His expression, presuming he could alter his features, seemed a perpetual scowl.

As he trudged into the room, each footfall reverberating despite the expensive carpeting, the auctioneer noted that there were two identical boxes strapped to his wide back, slung over his left shoulder with a chain. The boxes were metallic, covered in markings not that dissimilar to some of the objects he had just sold off. On the back of each was what was clearly a seal of some sort, perhaps from some long-forgotten foreign power. They were also vibrating.

Everyone scattered, giving the behemoth a wide berth. The screams continued to fill the air though the creature gave them no notice, striding purposefully to join the man. The auctioneer knew they were together and that the human commanded the beast.

"What gives you the right to do this?" He wasn't sure why he was suddenly so full of bravado, but the auctioneer also recognized that until the police turned up, he was Blackwood's presiding officer and as such, had to maintain the firm's dignity despite the unearthly scene before him.

The prince glanced in the auctioneer's direction, finally taking his rheumy eyes off the artifact in his grasp. One hand dipped fingers inside his belt and withdrew what appeared to be the remains of a dried plant. The fingers flicked and suddenly the desiccated thing was in the auctioneer's face and had sprung to life. The roots were attracted to the moistness of his mouth and reached in, tendrils growing by the second and forcing their way down his throat, filling the space and constricting his airway. He felt them cover his nose and snake up toward his eyes. Blind and unable to breathe, he panicked, hands now waving in the air.

He tried to clutch at the thing now alive inside his body. No matter how much strength was applied, the auctioneer could not remove the tendrils from his mouth and with every passing second, he lost strength. The man blacked out and toppled over, dead as he crashed to the ground.

Nuada glanced at the corpse, the tendril protruding from the slack mouth, ignoring the fresh rounds of screaming going on around him. He said to the people who were closest to him in a voice filled with pity—and scorn, "Proud, empty, hollow things that you are. You must be shown your place."

At that, a new sound filled the air, catching Nuada's attention. The man looked this way and that until he focused on the Pomeranian that had dared to growl, baring its teeth in his direction. He wanted to laugh at such a display of bravado from the weakest living being in the room, but could not find the mirth.

"May this remind you why you once feared the dark . . ."

He nodded and the troll removed the boxes, placing each on the carpet. They continued to vibrate, shaking back and forth, and sounds could be heard, mixing in with the screams and the dog's persistent growl.

Once on the ground, the circular symbol in the center of each rotated counterclockwise and then the panel slid up, revealing the contents to the shadowy room and its panicked patrons. Many pairs of eyes could be seen in the darkness within and then suddenly, they burst forward, emerging from the box into the shadowy room.

Nuada watched as they came forth, wide rows of teeth glinting in the dim emergency lighting, and they scattered around the room.

And finally, the prince smiled.

CHAPTER TWO

To anyone driving through the thick woods on the outskirts of the New Jersey state capitol, the low-slung building complex was nondescript. It looked municipal so no one would question the waste management company supposedly headquartered there. The curious might wonder why such a firm needed a decorative brazier with an eternal flame or seven-foot-high walls keeping the public from the cluster of buildings that seemed such a natural part of the local terrain or why it was located so far from the city or other populated centers in Mercer County.

Should someone actually want to brave the gates, they would most likely be politely turned away by uniformed security officers with an excuse crafted not to raise any suspicions. Were they to be so foolhardy to try and scale the walls, they would find the top lined with triple strands of ultra-thin razor wire.

Despite its attempts at innocuous camouflage, the entire complex was patrolled routinely by armed guards accompanied by specially trained German shepherds. Being the evening, searchlights swept beyond the barriers, the powerful beams scaring away even the curious native denizens of the woods.

Everything had been designed and constructed with as much consideration for keeping the general public away as it was for keeping its occupants safely within. It had been constructed decades earlier, constantly upgraded with cutting-edge technology, paid for from various government accounts that avoided congressional scrutiny. No one could find the B.P.R.D. listed in a government directory and its employees were carried on the payrolls of various departments until recently, when its budget was consolidated into an obscurely named line item during the formation of the Department of Homeland Security. Those working for the Bureau did so in private, secure in the knowledge that they were protected.

Deep in the headquarters was its largest room, accessed through a set of floor-to-ceiling doors set in a wood-paneled, curved entranceway. To the doors' right was the huge number 51 in tall metal. It had once been the office of Professor Broom and now was more memorial than anything else.

Perhaps the most protected member of the staff was the one who lived in a colossal aquarium located within the office used by the late Broom. Resembling a library, the aquarium had been designed to provide privacy for its occupant in addition to huge floor-to-ceiling glass panels that allowed him to converse with people on the opposite side. Architects had been conscious to make the space harmonious with the rest of the actual cavernous library which had doubled as Broom's office. Above the tank and tucked into most walls were shelves of books, most from Broom's private holdings, acquired through the years. The leather chairs were intended to be comfortable during long periods of reading, with recessed ceiling lighting in addition to well-placed lamps for added illumination. The dark wood paneling and fixtures were complemented by a wide red runner that ran from the circular alcove at one end, topped by a stone statue bathed in golden light, past the aquarium and to the far wall. In front of the four panes of thick glass were stands to allow for books or documents to be placed and read from within the tank.

Abe Sapien, a blue-skinned aquatic being that blended the best of sea and mammalian life, floated contentedly in the tank, supported by a cloud of bubbles. The room was filled with the sounds of Vivaldi. He could hear the lush strings through a specially waterproofed set of headphones. Sapien was taken by Antonio Vivaldi's music, specifically Concerto no. 3 in F Major, known to classical fans as "L'autunno" and more commonly called "Autumn."

Not that the man entering the library could recognize the piece or even know that it had been inspired by a particular sonnet when written in 1723. His musical taste began and ended in the mid–twentieth century and music was rather far from his mind. Instead, he was focused on the here and now and could never understand how anyone, man or fish, could just float there listening to the classics.

Nor did the man stop and wonder why the tank remained in the library since, after all, the man who most used the room, and therefore provided Abe with companionship, was gone.

All he knew was there was trouble. Again.

With his ring, he rapped against the glass, creating a rhythm that did not go at all with the string section currently playing. The harsh metallic sound was sharp and got its job done, like its owner.

The man reached out to the stereo system, a little less state of the art compared with the security setup, and abruptly cut off the symphony. He then looked again within the tank and saw he managed to get Abe's attention.

"Fishstick," Tom Manning, the FBI's liaison to the B.P.R.D., said. "We gotta talk." With that, he held up a manila folder in a plastic bag, the folder labeled TOP SECRET in bright red, and he pressed it against the side of the aquarium.

Abe Sapien blinked once and nodded in understanding. He went to the opposite side of his home and began preparing to join the surface world. To accomplish this, he needed to protect his skin and most essentially his eyes. First, he slipped on a pair of goggles that Broom had designed to retain water so Abe would not dry out. Next came the addition of a broad metal and rubber collar that were fitted to cover his gills, allowing him to replenish his supply of water, enabling him to breathe while away from his home.

Ready, the figure, with webbed hands, feet, and arms, entered an air dock that filled with water and then drained away, allowing him to enter the library. He allowed the remaining droplets of water to wick away from his scaly blue-gray skin before entering the room to speak with Manning.

Tom Manning stood impatiently but knew he had little choice. To talk comfortably with Abe Sapien meant waiting for him to emerge which was easier said than done. He preferred to talk face to face with his agents, even those with extraordinary telepathic capabilities. Manning paced the library, not at all appreciating the once-in-a-lifetime collection of literature on the paranormal. Instead, he fretted about his pension, his last failed investment, how badly cooked his lunch had been, and whether or not he'd still be employed by the end of the next pay period. He hoped so; he had a car payment coming due.

The folder was tapped against his leg, a nervous habit he had long since stopped trying to break. Instead, he let it beat against his off-the-rack pants and tried to avoid exploding the moment Sapien joined him.

Of all the freaks he had dealt with, he liked Abe the most. Sometimes they saw the world the same way and despite the amphibian's refined tastes, Manning couldn't help but see him as an ally, a kindred spirit, maybe even a friend.

Abe finally met with him, nodding his head in welcome, preferring not to attempt shaking hands. Manning could respect that and he took a deep breath to control his mounting anxiety. He was pleased when Abe gestured toward the folder, finally ready to discuss the matter.

With a snap of his meaty hands, Manning opened the folder to display prints of photographs depicting Hellboy. This was not in itself unusual but that they were taken of the large, red being running down a New York City street, his beloved, custom-made, high-caliber gun, nicknamed Samaritan, waving in the air—well, that was unusual.

"Undercover," Manning began without preamble. "Can't he get the meaning of the word? Fishstick, we are still government funded and . . . still a secret."

He paused, ready to admit something to his colleague. "A dirty secret if you ask me. Officially, we don't exist."

Abe looked and Manning hated that the agent had a face that was tough to read. His expression always seemed so . . . placid. But he seemed to get what Manning was ranting about, what he had fruitlessly complained about in the past. That in itself got him worked up and his words spilled out without much coherence.

"That's the problem when you . . . when you get . . . things like these . . ."

Abe once more took the photos and studied them, clearly allowing Manning to collect himself so the conversation could progress.

"Subway, highway, park . . . we suppress each photo," Manning managed. "Each . . . each . . . cell-phone videos . . . they cost me a fortune."

His arms waved through the air further expressing his dismay, radiating frustration with each motion. "And then they pop up on YouTube," he added. "God, I hate YouTube."

Abe nodded in sympathy and Manning took comfort in that. The explosion of viral videos on the Internet only complicated his job. At least at the outset. Later, he found a bunch of really useful techies at FBI headquarters further south in Washington, D.C. Most sightings were digitally modified or strategetically commented on, redirecting the online conversation away from whether or not a large, red demon ran freely in America. This was another urban legend, like Bigfoot—the stuff of *Weekly World News,* not CNN. That certainly helped mitigate the matter but the graphics continued to crop up like so much kudzu.

Abe finally spoke and his soft, almost melodious voice brought about a hard-to-find calm in Manning. Even if the words were ones he didn't want to hear.

"He wants the world outside to know," Abe began. "What we do. What he does."

Manning disagreed. "No, no. He loathes me." There was a plaintive tone in his voice that he disliked hearing but it was there nonetheless. This wasn't about Hellboy's desires, but about a vendetta.

Abe said, "I don't think so."

That set him off and Manning felt his anger rising, because as much as he might like Abe Sapien, he disliked the close friendship the fish-man shared with Hellboy. It felt too much like a betrayal.

"Oh, you don't?" the federal bureaucrat asked. He reached into his suit jacket and withdrew a crumpled, badly torn sheet of taupe paper. It was a target-practice poster with the usual bull's-eye and assorted concentric circles. What made this infuriating was that the rings were superimposed over a photograph of Manning's face. Holding it at eye level, he dangled it before Abe.

"Target practice. Then he posts them around . . . You know how I feel?"

All Abe could manage was, "Oh, dear."

Before either could say anything else, a roaring sound permeated the thick oak doors and walls of the library. Whatever was nearby was loud and rather unhappy. Manning was unused to the sound and flinched, concerned about what could ruin his day any further.

The two walked to the library door and opened it. Seeing nothing, but hearing the growl even more clearly, they walked down the metallic halls, which were as sterile as the library was warm and welcoming.

Rounding a corner, they entered what Manning had dubbed the Freak Corridor, the route taken by the B.P.R.D. security forces to corral and bag things that had no business being loose in the world. Sure enough, as they walked down the hall, three uniformed security guards grappled with a chained, netted and barely restrained creature. It was misshapen, seemed to possess three arms and legs, had four eyes, and seemed to secrete something glistening and goopy.

"What's going on?"

Abe didn't seem at all concerned about the growls and merely replied, "Oh, it's Friday."

Manning couldn't imagine how someone who spent so much time underwater, where sound always seemed muffled to him, could be so discerning out of his element. He tried to shrug it off and get back to the subject that mattered most to him.

The two paused their conversation to watch as a series of gleaming steel doors slid apart in a variety of directions to grant the team access to an inner chamber where the creature could be secured and subdued.

When the last door slid shut with a satisfying clang, Manning continued as if they hadn't been interrupted.

"I tell you, Fishstick: He hates me. He's out to destroy me."

He paused dramatically, allowing Abe a chance to tell him how wrong he was. His right hand reached into his pants pocket and withdrew a roll of Tums. With a quick motion, he unwrapped one, then two, and popped them into his mouth, chewing noisily. Abe didn't say a word to reassure him, sending Manning to a new level of despair.

"My street cred is low," he complained.

That seemed to earn a response. "Street cred—?"

The incredulous tone was evident and coming from Abe, which hurt. And earned Manning two more brightly colored Tums.

"My mojo," he emphasized. "Washington . . . they're wondering if I've got the . . . stuff?"

Again a pause, inviting Abe to comment. None came and Manning was ready to just call it a week. "You . . . you think I have an easy job?"

A fifth Tum found its way from wrapper to mouth.

"You think I just enjoy being—a—a—pain in the—neck? I'm . . . medicated . . ."

Abe stared at him, expectantly, ready to hear more about this new condition. Manning, who wasn't really medicated, just frustrated, waved the remaining roll of antacid tablets in the air, much as he had waved the photos not that long ago.

"This is not candy," he insisted. "It's—it's—antacid. It may be over-the-counter medication but it is . . . medication."

Abe politely watched him and Manning paused, realizing he may have been overreacting just a bit. While maybe not professionally medicated, he knew he was bone tired.

In a quieter tone, his weariness evident, Manning said, "I

worry . . . because . . . you know? I am—we are—after all, humble public servants . . ."

Whatever Abe was not saying, whatever was on his mind, seemed to finally bubble to the surface. He seized that moment to interject words into what had been for too long an unpleasant monologue.

"It's not about you," the agent said gently. "He's acting out. Things are a little tense with Liz."

Mention of Hellboy made sense, but how did Liz enter the conversation? Manning knew that the two had finally hooked up after too many years of them making puppy eyes at each other—he thought it would finally stop getting sickening but then the cooing couple seemed even worse to him. Still, someone else's unhappiness got him interested.

"Tense? Tense how?"

"Well," Abe began tentatively, seemingly uncertain how much to reveal about his friends. Manning clearly wanted to know it all and used the silence as a crowbar. "The usual—new couple—making adjustments—they argue . . ."

This seemed to work better than the antacids as the anxiety and fear that he had been feeling since the new round of photos had landed on his desk that afternoon faded. Just like that. To hear that Hellboy was suffering, at the hands of the woman he loved, was just too juicy to pass up.

"They do?"

Abe nodded. "Sometimes."

He had to know more. "How bad?"

"Good days and bad," Abe admitted, clearly uncomfortable at the questioning, but Manning just needed to know *everything*.

At that propitious moment, the concrete wall they were standing near rumbled then abruptly exploded, showering the hallway with chunks of concrete. Bits of stone and dust blew toward Manning, whose suit was now dirty and in need of dry cleaning, another bill he didn't need. He tamped down that depressing thought as he watched the cause of the explosion: Hellboy was being propelled through the wall.

Before he could land, a huge blue-white ball of flame engulfed him and blew off the remains of the metal door that had been set in the concrete.

Finally, Hellboy landed in a smoking heap at their feet. Bits of his clothing were still aflame and parts of his skin had been charred from red to black.

Manning felt welling glee rise from his soul but he knew better than to smile or even express any pleasure at the demon's predicament.

"Hey, Blue . . . Manning . . ." Hellboy casually said from the floor.

Manning liked being acknowledged like a pal, a genuine colleague.

Hellboy ignored them as he reached behind him, patting out the small flickers of fire that chewed away his black T-shirt. Satisfied the fire was gone, he rose and without a glance in their direction, strode back through the hole in the wall, returning to his private room and the source of the fire—Liz.

Manning wasn't sure if he should be disturbed, elated, or not, that such an explosion failed to trigger a security or fire alarm. He glanced questioningly at Abe.

All his friend could add was, "Then again, there are the *really* bad days."

CHAPTER THREE

Hellboy was still smoking as he returned to the remains of his room. Abe and Manning were forgotten as he focused on the figure rifling through his things. His prized possessions, collectors' items all. She was handling them without any respect, her lithe body still shimmering in blue flame.

God, she was a sexy thing.

Seeing her touching his things, though, that set him off anew. With more frustration than anger in his voice, he resumed their fight.

"I have one rule!" he yelled, raising a crimson forefinger. "Don't touch my stuff."

Liz finally looked up, an eight-track tape in one hand, a record album in the other; both seemed to smolder ever so slightly. She glared at him, incredulous. "That's your rule?"

He couldn't take his eyes off her, even when they were fighting. She was everything he wasn't: slim and delicate, stylish, with her dark, asymmetrical bob of a haircut and big eyes. Liz was made to be protected and he considered himself fortunate, even then, that she was his. But, there was a fight to win and he needed to make his points clearly before things spiraled even further out of control.

"The one and only. I'm easy." And he smiled at her.

She tossed the melted eight-track into the overflowing garbage can nearby. Hellboy walked over to retrieve it and several other items from his collection that Liz was far too eager to part with. He couldn't believe she would toss out Spike Jones or McCoy Tyner, let alone his Edgar Winter tapes. As he gathered up the castoffs, Hellboy glanced up and his gaze was caught by the various TVs which were set to various cable movie channels. On one was Whit Bissell talking with Julie Adams, both concerned over the *Creature from the Black Lagoon*, while the other had Mae Clarke pleading with Colin Clive to come to his senses in the original *Frankenstein*. Boy, they knew how to make movies back then, he mused.

His eyes traced the room and noted that she hadn't moved anything else. It had been an adjustment as her clothing, especially her shoes, fought for space. The clothes he understood, but the sheer volume of shoes seemed to double by the day and he couldn't begin to fathom why anyone needed so many styles of footwear. Oh well, he thought, love her, love her shoes.

As his eyes returned to the object of his affection, she was once more sorting through his extensive music collection. In one hand was the CD of *Gets Next to You* while the other held the original LP pressing.

Liz ticked them off dismissively, "Same record: CD . . . LP . . ."

He could not believe what he was hearing and knew he had to defend his collection, for what felt like the tenth time that day. To change the argument, he tried a more direct approach. "Al Green," he explained. "Can't listen to Al Green on a CD. But the CD's good to keep."

Liz stopped, blinked, and put down the CD. She reached for the next pile and pulled up the thick white plastic tape recording of the same album. With as much disbelief as she could muster, her voice rising, she said, "And an eight-track—*an eight-track!!!*"

Gently, so as not to lose yet another rare collectible, he pried the tape from her hand and placed it back with the others, far from the trash bin. He shrugged at her nonchalantly and added, "One day mankind will realize its mistake. Eight-track was the way to go!"

By then, Abe and Manning had quietly entered the room, watching the lovers' quarrel, and had kept silent. They remained near what had once been a doorway and wall and was now sized for a nice picture window if only the view was of anything but a steel corridor.

Having heard enough, Abe stepped forward, away from Manning and near his friend. Hellboy drew some pleasure from that and broke into a smile when he heard what the amphibian had to say.

"Much as I hate it," Abe admitted. "I have to agree with that."

As Liz gaped at him in amazement, Hellboy took a moment to break away from the argument and kneel down to peek under their king-sized bed. He saw pairs of eyes peering back at him, but out of reach.

"You can come out now," he said in a quiet tone, coaxing them on.

At that, nearly three dozen kittens of varying size, color, and species accepted the offer and charged from under the bed, adding a fur-covered element to the cacophony that was their living quarters. The mewling and crying noises drowned out Liz's anguished sounds and the audio coming from the televisions against the far wall.

Her shoulders sagging, Liz seemed ready to admit defeat and Hellboy suddenly felt sorry for her, and he also felt oddly in need of apologizing. He wasn't entirely sure why, probably something to do with his sympathy for her side of the argument even if he wasn't quite ready to concede anything.

Her eyes wet with tears that she refused to shed, Liz asked him plaintively, "What about me, Red? I need some space! Enough to find . . . to find . . . my toothbrush."

To prevent the tears, she flared up, flushing the room in pale blue light from her body.

Hellboy blinked at the display and then looked around quickly and said, "Toothbrush is right there."

"Where?" she challenged him.

As his hand pointed, Liz's eyes followed and she saw her toothbrush nowhere near the bathroom where it belonged, but instead, somehow stuck in a heap of cat kibble which had spilled from its container. Two of the kittens were standing there, nibbling away at the snack, shedding atop the brush.

"Right there—mmh," he said, finally realizing how out of place the toothbrush was and the depth of the problem they faced.

She wrinkled her nose in disgust and then her shoulders sagged. The fight seemed to drain out of her and Hellboy was ready to concede anything, whatever it took to make her happy. If only he was certain he knew what that might require.

"I can't live like this. Listen . . ." she began but her next words were cut off when the blare of the alarm sounded. The blues from her flame were replaced by the deep reds of the emergency alert system.

The call to action relieved Hellboy of having to deal with the fight, the mess, the cats, and the debate over eight-tracks, CDs, and LPs. Cats scattered in reaction to the shrill sound and he looked hopefully over at Manning and Abe. Though Manning often rubbed him the wrong way with his superior manner and substandard respect for the B.P.R.D. agents, neither looked like they had a clue as to what was summoning them at this hour.

The alarm actually brightened Hellboy's mood and he refused to examine what that meant. Instead, he looked at his lover apologetically. Carefully modulating his voice, he told her, "Oh—damn. Gotta go. We all gotta go, right?! That's an emergency. Right?"

He looked directly at Manning who nodded back; his full, round face and balding head shone with perspiration. The reddish lights were reflecting off it, making the human look as red as Hellboy was naturally. It didn't look nearly as good on Manning as it did on him.

While Manning spoke on a cell phone, yelling to be heard over the alarm, he led Liz, Abe, and Hellboy from the rubble that was the bedroom to the headquarters' locker room. Each agent silently recognized the time for personal gripes had passed and they were no longer appropriate. Instead, the alarm signaled they were needed because something beyond the control of normal law enforcement was in the vicinity. Most likely Manhattan, since monsters rarely came to Trenton.

Hellboy appreciated the break in the argument since it wasn't the first time they had bickered. It wasn't even the first time they had fought over his music collection or the mess that their combined belongings had generated. It was different, though. He knew it. She had reached a breaking point and that concerned him. He couldn't lose her, not again. When Liz Sherman first arrived at the B.P.R.D. it began a cycle of her working with them and then leaving. Her abilities and their devastating effect frightened her and cost her much in her young life. All through it though, they formed a friendship that deepened into a bond that at first felt like siblings, until he felt something deeper. Broom said it sounded to him like love, and that's when Hellboy knew he loved Liz and would go on loving her.

As he lost Broom, the man who raised him, he finally gained Liz and the tradeoff didn't seem fair but made him content. In those few months, the adjustment from friends to lovers was bumpier than he had ever imagined.

He would not lose her.

So lost in thought was he, that Hellboy went through the motions of preparation, having done this countless times through the years. The equipment and ordnance improved, got fancier and deadlier, but the drill was the same. As a result, he missed half of what Manning was telling them. It didn't really matter. Manning could usually be ignored and the summons told him all he needed to know: something big and ugly needed taking down. They were the ones to do it, especially Hellboy.

When Hellboy refocused on his surroundings, he spotted various agents bolting from the locker room to a line of waiting, gleaming black SUVs that screamed government but were supposed to be unobtrusive. He followed them from the locker room to his own assigned vehicle, a garbage truck. Within, it was a fully equipped mobile lab that was also designed to hide him and Abe given their nonconformist appearance.

As the truck's rear panel opened, the driver patiently awaiting his passengers, Manning finally walked over toward Hellboy. As usual, he looked grave and took the operation way too seriously as far as the demon was concerned. Manning came too close and Hellboy could smell the fruit-flavored Tums the fed favored.

"Now, listen," Manning said in that pompous voice. "We are going to downtown Manhattan, Red. Downtown. This is dangerous. Very dangerous. For you—and me."

He let the words linger and then looked steadily up into Hellboy's eyes. Beyond the sternness, he could see the concern, and even the fear. While normally dismissive of Manning, he was taken aback a bit by how much the human was worried. That wasn't good.

"I know you dream of the outside world. Trust me," Manning continued, "It's not that great. Savage, as a matter of fact. Bad."

He reached into his inner coat pocket and withdrew a fat, tightly wrapped olive green cigar. Gently, he raised it and placed the end, already neatly trimmed, into Hellboy's gaping mouth.

"These, on the other hand . . . are good." With that, Manning opened up a Zippo and lit the cigar, which Hellboy puffed on greedily, helping to get a good flame going. The first lungful of smoke was smooth, tasty, and better than the stogies he usually enjoyed. Happily, he nodded at Manning with approval.

"Cuban," the federal agent confided with a whisper.

"Mmh—Cuban." They could have been from Mars or Mongo for all he cared. It was good and it was free.

"We confiscated a box of these—I'll get you more," Manning continued. Once more he reached into his coat pocket and this time withdrew three more Cubans, casually placing them into a deep pocket in Hellboy's overcoat. As he did, patting them into place, Manning leaned once more toward his colleague.

"I want to ask you to be very, very, very . . ." he struggled for the necessary word.

"Discreet," Abe offered and Hellboy noticed his friend standing downwind of the cigar.

Manning merely glanced in Abe's direction and then returned his gaze to Hellboy. "Thank you. Discreet." He then reached into his pocket a final time and withdrew a cigar clearly intended to be enjoyed by the fed.

Hellboy got it. The cigars were buying his cooperation. He puffed happily, because right now, he wanted to be on good behavior for Liz. If Manning benefited, no big deal.

"Invisible," he agreed. "In and out." He puffed happily, proud of himself.

The bubble burst, though, when Liz's incredulous laugh rang through the air. Suddenly, the cigar wasn't so sweet, his confidence was turning to clay and his good mood was rapidly dissipating.

Turning on his heel, he looked wounded as he addressed Liz, who stood there, ready for the mission in her black B.P.R.D.-branded windbreaker, arms folded and an angry expression marring her amazing features.

"I can be discreet if I want to," he defiantly told her. "I followed you and Myers—didn't I?" It wasn't easy following the couple as he leapt from rooftop to rooftop on a cool evening nearly a year back, but he did and neither suspected the jealous demon was in the vicinity. He took great pride in that, especially since it worked out for the best. Myers, nice guy and all, was gone and Liz was his. Or was.

He needed her in his life.

Returning his attention to Manning, Hellboy proclaimed, "I'll be like a shadow."

With practiced ease, he lifted the cigar right from Manning's hand and added it to the stash in his pocket. Manning, knowing better than to challenge the demon, nodded with approval.

"I like that."

"Like a shadow in the night," Hellboy confirmed, climbing into the garbage truck. He paused and aimed his forefinger at Manning, cocked his thumb and fired an imaginary bullet in a rare act of camaraderie.

Pleased, Manning shot back using his own hand. As the door closed, Hellboy decided he didn't like the way Manning looked when he was happy. Or maybe he was just unused to seeing him smile.

CHAPTER FOUR

By the time the entourage of vehicles arrived across the bridge, Blackwood's Auction House was overrun with members of the various emergency response teams. Trucks and equipment from the police and fire departments littered the street while yellow tape crisscrossed the area, boxing out the public, especially the press. Swooping light from the pair of helicopters flying back and forth over the block added a surreal element to the night.

Worst of all, the rain had yet to let up.

Manning watched from the rear of the SUV as it snaked through traffic, escorted by two NYPD cars, and could already feel his night growing from bad to worse. First there was trouble with Hellboy and Liz—that meant coddling them both and keeping them focused on the matter at hand, not each other's hurt feelings. Boo hoo. They'd have to get over it on their own time.

Now they, and the fish-man, were here on the government's dime and were going to be expected to perform.

Without being seen, of course. For the last eighteen years, he had been the B.P.R.D.'s public face, handling the media and the occasionally curious politician. He was paying his dues, hoping his indiscretion in 1996 would be largely ignored as he worked the back channels of Washington and kept the right people happy while protecting Broom and his team of misfits. Manning knew the world faced some real, terrifying dangers. The most recent one, Rasputin, was just the latest in a long string of horrors that placed the planet on the brink of annihilation. Broom had taken the time to show him incident after incident dating through the ages. Humanity had to share the world with a startling variety of nonhuman life but was largely ignorant of its neighbors. Somehow, mankind always managed to conjure up a champion or two and keep malevolent beings at bay.

Today, that responsibility fell to the B.P.R.D. and it was one he did not take lightly despite disliking the duplicity the job required. Do a good enough job keeping the ghouls, goblins, and spooks in check and eventually he could be more visible, unlike his agents. The few members of the federal government who knew what he did for the B.P.R.D. would have to acknowledge his worth and allow him to leave with a perfectly good cover story and once again resume his political career. After all, his father sat at home, waiting for the chance to say, "My son, the senator."

He couldn't possibly disappoint his father, the former senator from Connecticut.

Still, with Broom now gone, Hellboy was becoming an increasing problem as his adolescent-like antics threatened to expose not only himself, but the entire operation. That, coupled with the horrendous dancing incident, would most likely permanently end his political aspirations.

So, once more into the breach or more likely, into the unknown. His briefing en route was hasty and garbled. The press would demand details and he'd have to make things up as he went along, keeping their attention on him—which was just fine by him—and let his agents do their jobs.

Discreetly. Please let it be discreetly.

Manning stepped from the SUV in a black raincoat, which was instantly dampened, while an agent held an umbrella over his head, failing to keep his balding head from getting wet. Now he'd glisten in the camera lights. He hated that.

No sooner did his feet touch the slick pavement than the pride of journalists rushed him. Cameras, microphones, and electronic doodads he did not recognize were thrust his way, everyone wanting their piece of the action. Noting the garbage truck had rolled into position, he was ready.

In his most authoritative, senatorial tone, Manning began his brief. "Earlier tonight," he told the mob, "U.S. Customs discovered a few illegally imported items: a minor infraction. And, um . . . a gas leak . . . they . . . detected a gas leak up there . . ."

"What sort of infraction?"

"Is it nuclear?"

"What country did the items come from?"

"What sort of gas? Is it sarin?"

Looking beyond them, he saw his men fan out, keeping up the pretense that they were the agents under his command. Well, they were, just not the ones he intended to talk about.

Ignoring the direct questions, he maintained his patter with earnest authority. "Now, FBI agents under my command have taken over the premises and an investigation is underway."

One particularly fetching-looking reporter, barely out of j-school no doubt, caught his eye and he nodded in her direction.

"Yes, Debra?"

As she asked her vapid question, Manning placed his right hand behind his back and crossed his fingers, in theory protecting him from being caught in a lie.

Now inside the building itself, entering from the service bay where trucks such as their refuse vehicle could park without question, Hellboy took Agent Marble with him to the main sales room while Abe and Liz led agents Steel and Flint down a corridor toward a storage room.

As they split, Hellboy noted Abe and Liz whispering among themselves.

Hellboy didn't mind them chatting—they were friends after all. He just didn't like what they were probably talking about. Him. And them. Hellboy was mindful that he needed things to go well that night so he had even a remote chance of smoothing things over with Liz before the sun rose. If things were allowed to fester, he feared he'd never make her happy again.

So, it was back to the mission.

The storage room they were in was large, filled with chairs that were anything but neatly stacked up. In fact, the storage room could have rivaled the quarters Liz and Hellboy shared in Trenton for messiness. That in itself told her something had happened here. Beyond the mess, though, there was no blood or ichor, no inappropriate smells, and most certainly no bodies.

Leaving the room, Agent Steel, muscular and prone to bad pick-up lines, climbed the nearest set of stairs. He was a good agent so she tolerated his lame attempts at humor. Usually all it took was one look to send him away. As Steel reached the top, he peered into an open walk-in vault that must have held the night's items *du jour*.

A hand signal indicated it was empty and not a danger. Abe signaled back and watched as Steel and Flint donned plasma-screen night-vision handheld scanners to better study the area. They waved their devices in a pattern, displaying patience and training that Liz had to admire. They were everything her lover was not. He was too impatient and impetuous on these sorts of missions, which exasperated her and no doubt drove Manning to drink.

A low rumble of thunder from outside could be heard, and made the darkened area seem even more ominous. That it was devoid of life only added to the tension she felt.

"Whatever they called us for is over," she said into her communications device. "We had over seventy guests reported but we have no survivors. No bodies. Nothing. Level above and below . . . cleared."

Hellboy hadn't bothered to learn what was for sale since he couldn't afford and most likely didn't want what they were offering. Standing in the center of the room, he saw chairs smashed, knocked over, and spilled in a random pattern. The blown-apart doors spoke of strength which had him concerned. It was the carnage born of chaos and he had no idea yet what had caused it.

Windows had been broken so rain mixed with the mess and in the dark, he had trouble telling blood from water—but the smell told him things were . . . off. At that, he cracked open the Samaritan and speed loaded it. He was determined to be ready.

"Same story here, babe," he confirmed into his communicator.

As he spoke, he watched Marble poke around a pile of debris and hold up what looked to be a diamond-studded dog collar. What a waste of money. The next item, though, was a bone—looked to be a femur and it also looked like whatever wore the collar used it for a chew toy.

"*Don't call me babe,*" she said and Hellboy shot a murderous glance at the smirking Marble. Geez, did everyone know he and Liz were having troubles?

Flustered, he quickly added, "I-I said *Abe*. Wrong channel." He slapped a thick finger against his earpiece before speaking again.

"Abe, I think Liz is still mad at me."

"*Same channel.*" She did not at all sound pleased.

He glanced up and saw Marble was eavesdropping so he shooed him away to investigate more debris so he could have just a touch of privacy.

"Oh." He also stepped away, creating more distance from the agent, who finally returned to his investigation. Hellboy ignored the mess around him, the danger that made his neck tingle, and focused on the one thing that meant anything to him.

"Can I ask you something?"

"*Yes?*"

Nervously looking around, he decided the agent assigned him was still too close. He waved his hand with more authority, then raised his voice to add, "Go look over there—willya, Marble?"

Hoping his order would be obeyed *and* would impress Liz with how seriously he was taking matters, he turned his back on the agent, lowered his voice and continued. "You . . . you still mad at me?"

"*You think?*" Two words, but dripping with months of pent-up pain, anger, and frustration. Not good, not good at all.

"Yeah—yeah. I can sense it. It's . . . it's . . . am I wrong . . . ?"

Before he could even finish the question, she already answered it. "*No.*"

He felt her slipping away. He couldn't lose her, not so soon, not after Broom had left him all alone. Whatever it took, he'd do it. Even if it meant dumping his collection. All of it. "When we get home . . . I'm gonna clean my mess up, okay?"

Hopefully, he waited for her approval.

"*That's not the problem.*" His shoulders sagged and he lowered the Samaritan, no longer caring about the danger that had summoned him to this ruin of an auction house.

His next words came out as a whisper, his pain evident. "Then, what?"

She couldn't believe they were having this conversation, here and now with them not even looking at one another. They were on a mission, standing in a building where something deadly had happened and whatever had caused it might still have been present.

Beyond the unknown, there was also the fact that their intimate issues were being overheard by others; in her case, Abe. He tried to look like he was investigating, but they both knew he was listening.

"Not now," she said, avoiding Abe's sympathetic stance and looking toward the ground. "I . . ."

Near her feet was a large rectangular box, made from some dense metal, perhaps iron. Training her scanner on it, she forgot about their lovers' quarrel and focused solely on the box. She saw symbols and the royal seal embossed into the metal. With the scanner she snapped an image and then popped out an instant print, a close-up of the seal, without having to disturb it.

Turning, she handed it over to Abe, who remained a respectful distance away, unaware of her discovery.

"Now this is interesting," she said to her friend.

Abe took the print and held it close to his goggled eyes and admired it.

"A royal seal," he began but his words were cut off by the arrival of scuttling feet against the room's floor. They sounded numerous and approaching with alarming speed. To his enhanced ears, they also sounded deadly.

"Guys," he announced, "We have company . . . burrowing creatures . . ."

He stopped in mid-sentence and quickly accessed the box of arcane books he carried with him. Abe wasn't one to use a lot of technology, more comfortable with words on paper than pixels on a screen. It had a lot to do with having been born back in the eighteenth century, she knew, but it also took him time to complete his research. Time they likely didn't have at that moment.

A webbed hand rapidly turned pages until Abe found what he sought. As he looked over at her once again she wished she could more easily read his non-expressions.

". . . with a very active metabolism."

That didn't sound promising at all. She felt the pit of her stomach turn cold, as if her inner furnace had suddenly snapped off, sapping her of the one edge she had should there be a fight. While Abe brought a certain level of comfort, right now she needed to have Hellboy's brawn here, too. Damn, she needed him.

"*How many of 'em?*"

Well, at least he was paying attention and taking this seriously.

"Many," Abe responded. He read for a moment more before asking, "have you noticed the floor?"

"*Uh . . . thick rug, light brown . . .*"

Abe interrupted him. "There is no rug."

"*Aw, crap!*"

"Precisely." He shared a look with Liz, who was somewhat amused at the image of Hellboy standing in an inch-thick pile of monster poo. It would serve him right and would be laughable except whatever could turn humans into excrement that quickly was a serious threat.

"There are no corpses because there are no leftovers," Abe explained. She never stopped marveling at how calm he always sounded, even with an imminent threat descending upon them. "All these things do is eat and eat—then *poop* and then eat again."

Liz, while horrified at the thought, couldn't resist being arch. "Remind you of anyone?"

"*What are you saying?*" Hellboy asked over the communicator, oblivious to her comment. "*That—that . . .*"

Abe finished the thought for him ". . . Some of New York's wealthiest have been turned into . . . excrement."

As he spoke, Liz spotted a poo-covered camcorder, one of the ones employed by the stewards during the actual auction. Gingerly, regretting having to touch it, she picked it up, swiped at it to clean it a bit and then hit the rewind button.

While she did that, Abe returned the book to the box strapped to his shoulder and resumed examining the storage room. His foot moved dirt and packing peanuts and broken furniture to the side.

He spotted something that discolored the flooring and studied it before pointing it out to Liz. "Dragging marks."

She nodded once in acknowledgement and then returned her focus to the camcorder. Having hit play halfway through rewinding, she was now skipping past the bidding until the attack began. There were voices, including one that filled her with dread. Then came the darkness, the emergency lights, and, almost simultaneously, the skittering sound and human screams. Silhouettes ran on and off camera; whoever held the recorder was also moving so she was getting nauseous trying to focus on what was happening, and what those creatures looked like.

In the sales room, monitors came to life and Liz's playback was suddenly illuminating the dim space. Instead of focusing on the muck that ruined his boots, Hellboy strained to see the culprits.

Just then, the angle abruptly changed as the camera clearly fell to the ground on its side. Craning his neck to straighten the image, Hellboy watched as a distinguished older man, once refined in his tux, was screaming, as he was pulled away from the camera by something that sounded rather insistent and hungry.

He cut the signal and resumed scanning the room with a flashlight. Now he knew what to listen for, but he wanted to see what could cause the carnage. The pale yellow light swept the area, illuminating cracks in the wall, rips in the carpet, torn furniture, and no monsters.

"Damn it, Abe! *What are these things?*"

The telltale sound of the creatures caught his attention and if Abe answered, he didn't hear it. Instead, he whipped around and aimed his big gun at a wall with a large—and growing—crack in it. All it took was one shot to widen the gap and allow him access.

Moving quickly, Hellboy reached the wall and stuck his sizable head inside and saw shapes burrowing through the plaster and wood, away from him and indistinguishable. So close, but not yet squishable.

"*Carcharodon calcerea,*" Abe recited from another book. Liz never ceased to be amazed how he knew which books he need-ed and was never caught short. That was a power unto itself.

"*Aw—geez—English . . .*" Hellboy pleaded over their open channel.

Abe stole a look at Liz before replying. She had put away the camcorder, sickened by what she saw and what she imag-ined happened off camera. All she wanted to do was go back to B.P.R.D. headquarters and not have to deal with this. She had enough problems to contend with and right now, she felt very sick to her stomach.

"Um. They're . . . tooth fairies." For a change, she could read his body language; Abe was almost embarrassed.

"*Ha,*" Hellboy laughed, more like a single bark.

Abe shook his head, despite Hellboy being far from sight. He held out the book to Liz, so she could see what he was talking about, seeking her validation. "No—no," he explained. "Third century, Black Forest. Feed mostly on calcium, bones, caulk, limestone . . . but they do go for the teeth first. Hence the name 'tooth fairies.'"

A sound caught Liz's attention and she tore her eyes away from the watercolor picture in the book. Instead, she focused her attention on the sound, isolating it. As she searched, she flexed her right hand and in the palm a small red fire flickered to life, heating up by the second. Soon it became a blue light creating an aura around the hand, coruscating as she focused her mind.

"Betcha they don't leave money either," she added dryly.

With her other hand, she waved the scanner in the same direction as the sound and found a variety of moving shapes within the wall. She tried to count the figures but their constant motion made that impossible so she stepped forward to get a better reading. So focused was she on the scanner that she didn't notice the wall crack, then splinter, until it finally exploded open, showering bits of plaster and wood ahead of the creatures.

Abe reached out to put himself between Liz and the creatures, a noble protective gesture. Not that he was any stronger or more capable, but still a nice effort. His webbed fingers pushed her back, touching her stomach. The effort alarmed her and she swatted the hand away.

"Oh, my god," Abe exclaimed. "Liz, you're pregnant."

Suddenly defensive, Liz protested, "No. I'm not sure."

A new set of feelings washed over her as she said that, the one thing she couldn't think about now suddenly foremost in her mind. She momentarily forgot about the creatures that had continued to break through the wall and would swarm over them in moments. She forgot about her fight with Hellboy and the kibble-covered toothbrush. All she saw in her mind's eye was a newborn infant, bathed in blue light from her fire, its skin bright red in honor of its father. So small, so vulnerable.

"You are."

In the sales room, Agent Marble, someone Hellboy barely knew, was near a different wall, with a web of cracks from top to bottom. He swung his flashlight back and forth, seeking additional evidence. The powerful light landed on something small and most definitely not human. In its clawed hands was a bone and the creature was happily gnawing on it.

"Hey, this guy is cute! Are you scared, little buddy?"

Hellboy turned to see the agent approach closer, the light more focused on the thing. To him, it appeared part plant, part insect, with at least four legs with skin that seemed supple. On closer study, he realized the gray hands ended in sharp tips; there were no claws, just one unit. The sticklike arms and legs supported a relatively tiny midsection. As Marble drew closer, the creature looked at him without moving. Then it seemed to flex a bit and translucent wings appeared—so yeah, it could fly like a tooth fairy.

As Marble drew closer, it saw the man and reacted like a scared, cute little thing. It retreated behind a fallen chunk of wall, just a little bigger than its body.

Remembering Abe's description, Hellboy called out, "No, don't . . . !"

But Marble seemed fascinated and didn't react to the warning. He continued to approach the creature, smiling and starting to extend a hand toward it, trying to coax it from hiding.

The creature actually responded and darn if it didn't look cute and nonthreatening right then.

Hellboy called again and this time caught Marble's attention. The agent turned, breaking eye contact with the creature. Hellboy signaled for the agent to come his way and then he looked again at the creature. That cute look was replaced with one that looked perturbed. In fact, its wings started to flutter and with every beat, the visage altered from benign to annoyed to angry; or was it hungry? Abe did say these things lived to eat.

The gray-green thing took to the air, opening its mouth until it got wider and wider, baring two rows of large square white teeth. It flew right at the agent who was backing away, finally recognizing the danger he was in.

Hellboy began to move, stepping over poo, broken chair legs, and bones, trying to pick up speed without slipping and falling. He couldn't risk firing his gun, not with the target so small and Marble in the way.

Powerless, Hellboy skidded to a stop, sliding in the brownish muck, but remained upright. His left hand raised the Samaritan and he waited.

The tooth fairy, though, continued toward Marble, gaining speed until there was impact. From across the room, Hellboy heard the wet sounds of chewing and the screams coming from the agent. That damned creature was trying to burrow inside his stomach, like they must have bored into the walls. The thing was trying to eat him from the inside and there was nothing Marble or Hellboy could do.

Screaming curses filled the room, drowning out the smacking sounds of the creature at work. Marble writhed in pain, struggling to withstand the assault to his organs until it got to be too much and he fell to his knees, splashing himself in the waste that had once been earlier victims.

Seeing the agent in such pain finally got Hellboy moving and he closed the distance until he grabbed hold of Marble. Enveloping the man in his arms, he reached his oversized right hand, wrapped in a glove, around Marble until he found the tooth fairy. With a single yank, he managed to pull the gnawing monster from the man's body. The removal brought forth sounds of complaint from the buzzing fairy and new screams of pain from the agent who thoughtfully passed out from the trauma.

Without stopping to study it close-up, Hellboy grasped the thing in his hand and crushed it to pulp.

By then, though, the fairy's family, friends, and acquaintances came pouring through the walls in numbers that staggered his vast imagination.

This was trouble with a capital T. Which rhymed with P which stood for poo.

The communications cut from Hellboy, Liz was able to focus on the fact that her fears were being made manifest. Abe knew. And if Abe knew then it must be true and she would have to deal with it.

That is, if she survived the night. The video had shaken her more than she wanted to let on. She was tougher now, a full-fledged member of the B.P.R.D., no longer prone to running away after each mission. She had a job, a home, a lover . . . she should have been content.

So why wasn't she?

Abe walked ahead of Liz, aiming his light forward. As he passed her, he said quietly, "You should tell Red."

"Drop it," she replied. Now was most certainly not the time, nor was she really ready for this conversation.

"What are you afraid of?"

Oh, she thought, you know, the idea of being pregnant when I have to fight creepies, the idea of raising a child with a man I can barely live with now, the concept of a demon/human hybrid making the baby an instant outcast.

But, before she could even attempt to put those thoughts into words, her flashlight beam found the source of the sounds that had been steadily growing. A tidal wave of green-gray winged beasts raced into the room, seeking their next meal.

In unison, Abe and Liz grabbed their B.P.R.D.-issued guns, which could shoot bullets or other deadly loads. They fired blindly before them, knowing the volume of tooth fairies meant they couldn't help but hit targets. Abe was the better shot, but he easily had a century of practice on her.

She ducked behind a large container and reloaded as quickly as she knew how, shoving any thoughts of the new life growing inside her to the side. Right now, she had to put a crimp in the creatures' dinner plans, and fast. Ready, she wrapped both hands around the butt of the gun and quickly rolled to her left, around the corner, and shot from a low angle, certain to get more of them.

Neither were carrying much in the way of ammunition and they'd run out long before the fairies did. She had one other weapon at her disposal but it required a great deal of calm and concentration to employ it. Now wasn't exactly the best time for either but she knew there was little choice.

"Steel. Abe," she called out, trying to be heard beyond the buzzing the creatures' collective wings were generating. "That safe. Can you make it?"

Abe paused after firing another round and looked at the vault atop the stairs. He instantly understood her plan and began trying to move but found his pathway blocked.

"I think so. But I need a clearing."

The ceiling above them disintegrated and they were showered with additional debris that served to scatter some of the tooth fairies. Pieces went splash in the muck, others bounced off Liz's head, making her wince. The cause, though, made her smile ever so slightly. Coming through the ceiling was first a great stone statue of some ancient goddess she did not recognize. Right behind it was Hellboy, arms flailing, the Samaritan waving up and down. Several fairies fell with him, but took to the air, getting off of the huge form. As he hit the ground, he managed to clear the very path Abe and Agent Steel needed.

She had to give her man credit. His mind was clear in a fight, knowing exactly what needed doing and who needed to do it. He barely had time to assess the situation but had correctly reached the same decision she had but did it in a fraction of the time.

They locked eyes and he said in an urgent tone, "Baby, you'll have to do it."

Liz nodded in agreement and closed her eyes, certain none of the flying menaces would threaten her. Not with Hellboy by her side. She focused on the energy that never really extinguished itself within her. It was like opening a box and letting it breathe fresh air, growing with power.

"Move away from the window," she commanded Hellboy and didn't pause to see if he'd obey. Of course he would—this was when he was at his best.

More to herself than anyone else, Liz whispered, "Fire is not my enemy." It was a mantra to control the raw power she was about to unleash. Liz could feel it leach though her pores, a white-blue aura of flame, generating tremendous heat. It would warm the room, put the tooth fairies on notice.

Louder and with greater emphasis to the words, displaying confidence she drew from her lover, Liz said, "Fire is in me."

Her brightening light spread out, suddenly coating the room in a warm, blue glow. As a result, they could now see that the stairs were carpeted with tooth fairies. Still, the agents had little choice to brave the path in order to reach the vault.

Abe and Steel charged up the stairs, bathed in her deceptively gentle blue light. They reached the vault and their flashlights urgently checked to make sure it was fairy-free. Before they could enter, a swarm of tooth fairies attacked from the stairs and grabbed on to Steel with surprising force. He was dragged back, his screams alerting Abe to the danger. The amphibian hustled forward, recognizing he lacked the ability to stop the creatures or save his fellow agent. Steel screamed and tried to fight back but there were far too many and they overwhelmed him, tumbling to the bottom of the stairs, his body disappearing into the mass of writhing, hungry beasts, each wanting a taste.

Undaunted by her warmth, the fairies closest to Liz began to approach her and then actually tried to scale her legs. Despite the fire being generated more seemed encouraged to pile on. Their mistake, she thought.

"Fire is mine," she continued, her voice rising. Urgently, she looked at Hellboy and then focused on the window. "Red," she warned in a harsh whisper.

Hellboy, though, did not seek safety from her impending flare. Instead, he positioned himself in front of the storage-room window and smiled at her. Oh no, she realized—this was another impetuous act, one that would complicate what she thought could get no more complicated. There was no time to discuss it, no time even to feel anger. Instead, she concentrated entirely on the surging energy welling up from toe to head.

She vaguely heard him say, "World, here I come."

Liz repeated, "Fire is me."

And then she went nova.

The room and its contents were instantly engulfed in a blue-white fireball that increased in size, volume, and force. Furniture and boxes were gone in an instant. Steel's remains were cremated along with the bodies of countless tooth fairies that clearly had no idea who they were dealing with. Walls were scorched and the flames raced from corner to corner, racing up the staircase and reaching the vault. Abe had managed to close it in time, but the force of the blast dented even the heavy steel in many places.

The concussive force blew Hellboy back before it could singe him, and he went hurtling through the glass window, out into the wet night air, exposed high above the police, and worse, the reporters.

Liz's fire caught up with him and he was encased in flame, his clothes catching fire, turning him into a fireball that now threatened the people below.

Was that a smile, Manning asked himself, a sense of dread filling him much the way fire filled Agent Sherman. Was that overgrown demon actually smiling? He hoped Hellboy burned.

Manning blinked then realized there was more than just Hellboy burning. He was coated in something, little beasties with wings. They were burning, too. Good.

A moment later, the smoldering B.P.R.D. agent landed with a crushing thud atop a police car, smashing the lights and siren, denting the roof, breaking all the glass.

Then Manning noticed all the people scattering. Cops went for their guns, reporters extended mikes, camera lights trained on the smoking figure, now being showered with additional debris that fell from the broken window like dirty confetti.

No one made a sound, staring in wordless surprise.

Manning gestured for the police, currently under his authority, to lower their guns. As they did, the dam broke and a torrent of questions flooded toward him. He turned his back on Hellboy, imagined his political career headed toward a sewer and then noisily gulped once and addressed the assembled, ravenous media.

"We, uh . . . have detected a, um . . . a gas pocket . . . inside there . . ."

He was instantly ignored, irrelevant, and the reporters surged ahead, toward the burning building and the bizarre figure still smoking atop the police car.

"Hey guys, guys, come back!!" Manning cried in a plaintive tone.

As the reporters neared Hellboy, though, Manning spotted that some of that debris was still moving. In fact, still alive. Tooth fairies were now loose in Manhattan. The sewer in his mind turned into a toilet and a flushing sound echoed in his head.

The hungry pack of journalists stopped short when they, too, noticed that the creatures were still alive. They snarled, showing their huge teeth, sizing up the human smorgasbord that awaited them. It was a tense standoff as cameras clicked, flashes went off, and creatures stared back, uncertain who to eat first.

Finally, one brave tooth fairy leapt ahead of the others, its wings beating furiously, as it made a direct approach toward a woman who needed to shed a few pounds, use a little less makeup, and, most immediately, run away.

A loud, thundering sound interrupted Manning's thoughts and he watched as the attacker suddenly blew apart in a greenish explosion of guts. He knew that sound. Hellboy had fired the Samaritan. Okay, that meant he wasn't dead, like Manning's career, so in the short term that was a good thing. Hellboy could protect the humans from the beasties. It also meant he'd be around to be killed by Manning later.

Several more shots from the oversized pistol resounded through the air and the remaining creatures were obliterated.

Manning allowed himself to turn and stare in disbelief. Hellboy stood there, unharmed, just charred, and casually plucked the remaining tooth fairy off his ruined overcoat. The thing wriggled upside down, struggling to fly away, no longer hungry but scared.

And then he grinned.

Hellboy dared to look right at the mass of cameras, including live feeds, and smile. He was enjoying this, finally out, no longer consigned to urban-legend status.

Now it was Manning's turn to boil and explode, much as Liz did four floors above them. He charged forward toward Hellboy, the cameras momentarily forgotten.

"What. Have. You. Done?"

Hellboy merely shrugged, not at all apologetic.

"I guess we're out."

CHAPTER FIVE

New Yorkers are often described as jaded. They take things for granted and immediately develop a blasé attitude toward people and places that others hold in awe their entire lives. It could be because the city enjoyed its status as the nation's first capital and rose to prominence for shipping and commerce. Its history was littered with major events and became a focal point, so people around the world first thought of New York, not Washington, D.C., when thinking of the new country.

Rapidly, the city became not only a financial center but all that money fueled the growth of cultural arts, restaurants, and larger-than-life figures. When sports became a predominant pastime, New York had to be the center. It's why Colonel Rupert paid an obscene sum to obtain a pitcher from Boston named Babe Ruth. It's why athletes, when they signed with a team or arrived via trade, always said it was their dream to play for the New York (Fill in the Blank)s.

Yankee Stadium and Madison Square Garden stood next to St. Patrick's Cathedral as cultural landmarks that had to be seen by those making a pilgrimage to New York.

Grand Central Station, back in the heyday of transcontinental railroads, was considered the crossroads of the world. And once New York became acknowledged as the center, people played it up with structures like the Empire State Building and then Rockefeller Center.

It also meant so many people and events occurred that attention spans shrank. Politicians, Broadway stars, authors, and even party-goers rose and fell faster than the Dow Jones average as people were assaulted with new, new, new.

Nothing prepared New Yorkers, though, for Hellboy and Abe Sapien. They looked unlike any athlete, singer, drinker, or patron of the arts that they had ever seen before. People sat in bars or their townhouses and gaped at the television coverage. At first, all they knew was that something horrific had happened at an auction house. Disasters were as plentiful as celebrities in New York, so there was morbid curiosity but nothing more.

Then came the explosion. Few New Yorkers got to watch carnage live, so curiosity turned to intense focus.

Those at the scene—reporters, onlookers, police, sanitation employees, firemen, and the homeless—gaped. Hellboy might have seemed like some movie monster on a bar TV, but it was something else to see him come crashing down, unharmed, and then casually fire the baddest-ass pistol ever witnessed to strike down hideous things. They stared in wonderment.

He smiled back.

The smile, the attitude, the lack of fear won the people over. Whatever he was, this red-skinned guy clearly arrived to kick butt and win.

Reporters screamed questions at him, but he said nothing in response. Grinning broadly, he waved at them and their cameras, beaming images across the country as more and more channels interrupted their programming to air scenes of this unusual event. News anchors fell over themselves to assess what had happened and who this demonlike being was.

Cheers were picked up by microphones, instructing the country that this was someone not to be feared but welcomed to the pantheon of champions.

The passersby and those who managed to escape the auction house before being consumed now waved whatever paper they had or could scrounge and demanded autographs. While Hellboy wouldn't talk to reporters, he did lean over the yellow police tape and begin scrawling as people gaped at the over-sized right hand and rocklike ring that surrounded it.

People reached out to touch the skin, which still smoldered a bit, watching raindrops hissing into steam on contact. He let them touch and continued to enjoy the moment, signaling he was no threat.

Within minutes, a new rush of sound was created when Liz and Abe staggered out of the building. Liz hung back, but was still caught on camera, from a variety of angles, and her beauty meant the cameras lingered as much on her as on Abe. Manning also hung back, fuming and trying to actually avoid the cameras for the first time in a decade.

Abe, Liz, and Hellboy exchanged hand signs and looks but what was being communicated was lost in the hubbub. At first Hellboy waved them over, but Liz quickly shook her head and stood in the back. Abe shook his head no, as well, but jerked a webbed hand toward the rear of the building.

Clearly, the rain interrupted productive signing, and the screaming questions from journalists were spoiling the moment, so it was time to go. Hellboy waved to the crowds, relishing the instant adulation, and backed toward Manning. One look from the fed, though, indicated a different direction was in order.

Hellboy began moving toward the rear of the building where Abe and Liz had gone to the garbage truck. The crowd followed, growing in number as neighbors left their homes and braved the rain. Taxis stopped as more people emerged and the crowed swelled further.

Away from the police barricades, the people drew closer and Hellboy did nothing to stop them. Neither did Abe, who seemed fascinated and pleased that his appearance, exacerbated by the necessary goggles and breathing collar, did not scare them away. Only Liz, the most human of them all, shrank away.

Uncaring that more secrets were being revealed, Hellboy led the trio into the garbage truck, its driver at the ready. Once aboard, Abe waved to the people as they pulled away and headed off into the night.

Bloggers and news writers for the Internet were the first, as usual, to link Hellboy to the grainy, blurry images that had been posted during the last decade. It was less than twenty minutes before a pic of Hellboy was posted next to one of Bigfoot with the headline: Separated at Birth?

Web metrics for any site related to urban legends, conspiracy theories, and religious zealotry reached new records that night.

Ratings for CNN and Fox News soared while local news covered every angle imaginable despite it being the overnight hours when few were thought to be watching. The city, though, never slept, and was awake to welcome its latest darlings.

By the thirty-minute mark, religious pundits claimed the building had exploded because hell had come to earth and Hellboy was its vanguard. The End Times were now.

CHAPTER SIX

West Side Rail yards
Midnight

The acres of train tracks where subways and trains resided when off duty had fallen into disuse and disrepair. Stretching from 30th to 34th streets on Manhattan's west side, they also proved increasingly tempting for developers, real estate magnates, and politicians. Considered the last stretch of Manhattan that could be rebuilt from the ground up, it was too tempting to allow the area to remain fallow forever. As a result, competing bids clamored for attention for everything from a new football stadium to lure the Jets back from New Jersey to a complex of residential and retail buildings. While the salivating people tried to outbid one another to gain control of the property, none were aware of who already held dominion over the space. To mere mortals, it was valued at six hundred to seven hundred million. To its residents, it was priceless and worth fighting to preserve.

One billboard, trying to sway the competition, already boasted that the Three Points Shopping Mall was coming. The picture featured a smiling Caucasian family wearing clothes that told you it was not going to be affordable for all of New

York's citizens. Staring at the sign in disgust was Prince Nuada, with Wink a dutiful step behind him. The prince was comforted by the weight of the night's prize and coldly smiled in return at the picture, knowing it was never going to happen.

With minimal effort, the prince vaulted a chainlink fence that was designed to keep mere mortals out, not those of superior stock. Wink followed soundlessly and then with one blow, smashed the fence, ripping it apart.

They strolled through the abandoned rail area to the tremendous roundhouse, the terminus where trains came and were spun into an appropriate direction for their next journey. Moonlight and rain fell through cracks in the ceiling but Nuada did not pause to admire the former or brush off the latter. He was there on grim business and wanted to just get on with it.

Of course, first there were protocols to be observed. The first such was approaching him now. A wizened old chamberlain, a man Nuada had known since birth, approached the duo and bowed low.

"Prince Nuada, your majesty, you honor us with your return," the man said in a voice rough with age, using Gaeilge, the ancient language of their people. "King Balor awaits you. But, uh, before entering the council chamber you must—as you must remember—uh, surrender your weapon."

To emphasize the chamberlain's point, a dozen butcher guards emerged from the gloom and stood in rows flanking the entranceway to the throne room. Each wore identical long white hair and was clad in dark, flowing robes. They carried with them weapons that were sharp and well polished. With military precision, they surrounded the Prince, making their intent clear.

"I will not." Nuada, too, spoke in the ageless tongue. He also paused to slowly withdraw his sword, which reflected the moonlight, the glimmer bouncing off several of the guards.

He then pointed the sword's tip against the chamberlain's throat, his expression hardening despite their years of familiarity with one another. He could not afford to appear weak, not when his time had come.

"It is the protocol, sire. For peasant and prince alike," the chamberlain continued, unfazed by the danger touching his skin.

"It will be my pleasure to finish you off, Chamberlain," Nuada said with firm conviction. His eyes ignored the guards that surrounded him, cutting him off from Wink's assistance.

The moments ticked in silence as it became clear neither prince nor chamberlain was about to concede.

The decision was taken out of his hands when a familiar voice came from the shadows behind him. He felt his heart lighten, his burden grow more bearable and he even allowed himself the briefest of smiles.

"Please, brother; surrender it."

He slowly turned his head to find Nuala, the sister he had not seen in far too long. She emerged into the moonlight and stood several feet from him. He appraised her, noting she looked much the same, willowy, hauntingly beautiful—and his identical match. The light put the facial scar or tattoo, a match to his own, into focus, and while to some it might have marred her beauty, he thought it made her uniquely attractive. Unlike his somber attire, her robes were a dusky blue with a wide golden belt.

Their eyes met for a beat. Then, finally, Nuada lowered his sword and returned his attention to the old man.

"For you, my sister, anything . . ." he said to her, but looked at the chamberlain and his guards.

With a flourish, he flipped the sword over and offered the hilt to a guard, who took it with a nod of approval. Nuada then straightened his broad shoulders and nodded his head toward his companion.

"Mr. Wink, however, cannot dispose of his weapon."

The flip comment was ill received by the chamberlain but Wink snorted with delight. After all, his tremendous strength and clawed hands were how he had been born. The right hand which was an artificial construct and connected to his arm could not be so easily turned over for safekeeping.

The ceremonial nonsense done, Nuada grew impatient to proceed deeper into the rail yards, to confront his father and put things into motion; things that once begun, could not be halted. Even by his sister's sweet voice.

The time had come for a reckoning.

CHAPTER SEVEN

"According to multiple eyewitnesses, lives were, in fact, endangered. To many, the explosion, which rocked midtown Manhattan, revealed the enormity of this government conspiracy. And its lengthy history: the Hellboy has been undercover for decades. Our investigative team has prepared a report on the most outrageous claims and how, sadly, most of them have come to be substantiated over the years."

The dark-suited, well-coiffed man suddenly vanished as the channel on the television monitor abruptly changed. The next image was of a dark-suited, well-coiffed man who was maybe a decade older than his predecessor. With a grim visage, he addressed the camera in a tone that threatened blood and thunder.

"They came from our pockets, that's where. Taxpayers' money. How can we, in good conscience, allow this to happen? What do we know about these creatures? How exactly are they better than the monsters they fight? What interests are they really protecting? What do they have to hide? I am prepared to go face to face with danger, so don't go away!"

Hellboy grew bored and ignored the command and flipped to the next channel. This time it was a woman, equally as well groomed as the others but prettier and in a dress that at least boasted some color. Behind her shoulder was a screen showing footage from the previous night.

"Most of the building suffered structural damage and the loss in antiques and valuables has been tallied, possibly, in the millions," she intoned. "But this was not the biggest news item."

Now the footage switched to a close-up of Hellboy, right after he had dispatched the final tooth fairy, and he was grinning with pleasure. "The final confirmation of an urban legend has left America in shock. Hellboy has emerged. He has stepped into the limelight."

Hellboy smiled at the television then looked around his room, with the gaping hole in the wall and the same clutter from the day before. He was delighted by the events and couldn't resist keeping his televisions tuned to the cable news channels with their round-the-clock coverage. With nervous energy, he kept flipping the second he grew bored by the pronouncements.

Fuming directly behind him was Manning while Abe was near the bathroom. Within the bathroom, Liz sat, avoiding everyone and that gnawed at Hellboy, causing him to remain focused on the televisions.

One screen cut to a cable newscaster who repeated all the same information from last night but this time the footage was not of Hellboy but of Manning discussing the, er, gas mains.

"Dear God," he muttered although Hellboy chose to ignore the walking pain in the ass. No more could Manning keep him away from the public. He felt free, free to do his job without skulking around and free to squire Liz around the city which might repair their strained relationship.

He never once paused to think about the tooth fairies and what would have sent them to the auction house.

"Hey, guys," Hellboy yelled over his shoulder. "You're missing this!"

Abe didn't seem to care. Instead, he moved closer to the bathroom door, which had remained closed since he had arrived some time before. Finally, summoning some courage, he knocked gently on the wooden door.

"Liz," he called in his soft, cultured voice. "Liz, are you all right?"

When she did not reply, he grew concerned and finally touched the door again, this time spreading his webbed hand out against the wood, psychically probing through it, to check on Liz.

What Hellboy did not realize at the moment was that Liz was within, staring at a pregnancy test stick. Sometime after she had permanently returned to the B.P.R.D., Manning saw to it that female agents were available to assist Liz as required. One had been quietly contacted to pick up a variety of medical and first-aid supplies, including a carton of pregnancy testers which, she said, Manning required for all personnel.

When they returned from the Manhattan mission, she went to the infirmary on her own and helped herself to a handful of the testers, ignoring the protocol to sign them out for inventory purposes. No one needed to know who took them, especially given the why.

Staring at the damp stick, willing the chemical test to hurry up, Liz said, "I'll be out in a minute . . ."

There. The result was becoming clear and sure enough, it was as she had expected.

"You don't need to do that," Abe said through the door. "You can trust me." Of course she trusted him. In fact, she trusted him with her life, him and Hellboy. No one else. He was everything Hellboy wasn't and the best friend a freak could want. Still, she had to see empirical evidence for herself, to put his psychic sensations into stark reality.

"Shut up, Abe," she said sharply. "And move your damn hand away from the door."

Pink. Positive. She was pregnant.

Well, she had known that from the moment Abe had confirmed her own suspicions. A woman could tell and for a few days, she had suspected as much which made her especially brittle when the last fight with her lover had ignited. Then Abe had sensed the new life growing within her and now the stick made it real.

Again. She placed it next to three other identically pink sticks.

Fear consuming her thoughts, she opened a fifth wrapper.

Hellboy continued to revel in the media exposure, totally ignoring the drama behind him. He didn't even mind watching Manning squirm—that was an extra bonus. With a press of the remote, some anonymous pundit vanished, replaced with the more pleasant and human look of Jimmy Kimmel. His late night show was having a field day with Hellboy and Abe so Hellboy settled back in his chair, relaxing his grip on the remote, and watched with delight, unwrapping a fresh candy bar.

On the screen, Kimmel had a photo of Hellboy next to him and was clearly riffing on how he had appeared.

"There you have it—*Hellboy*. Is he really . . . on our side?" Kimmel asked ominously. "I mean, he's bright red, has a tail and shaves his horns—horns, ladies and gentlemen. Horns are *never* a good sign."

The live audience guffawed at the devilish implications, in on the joke. The screen was split with an image of Hellboy next to a checklist. The word "Horns" appeared and then the word "check" alongside it. It was met with applause.

Hellboy chuckled and unwrapped a fresh Baby Ruth bar, munching away during his onscreen dissection. The white wrapper fell, joining a growing mountain of identical garbage. He was matching Liz candy bar for pregnancy test, but remained blissfully ignorant of the parallel.

"And what about this guy?" The screen cut to a picture of Abe from the previous night. It was a close headshot so the thick ribbed respirator system made him look even more unearthly. Manning groaned aloud.

"Walking around with a toilet seat around his head," Kimmel noted with a smirk.

The screen returned to the checklist, this time with Abe's image and the words "toilet seat" flashed, followed by the "check."

From across the room came the exasperated and not unexpected comment, "It's a breathing apparatus!"

Hellboy shared an amused look with Manning, although the federal agent didn't seem anywhere near entertained. Dismissing the man, Hellboy looked over at Abe, who lingered near the door. This was his day, and Hellboy wasn't going to let anything ruin his buoyant mood.

"We should get rid of the garbage truck, too," Hellboy announced. Manning and Abe stared at him with incredulous looks, or at least Abe's body language signaled surprise. "It sends the wrong message."

Abe stepped forward, hands spread apart. "You . . . you think that's our problem? Transportation?"

Hellboy was about to reply but instead, he glanced back at the television and was caught by the shot of Liz. God, she was gorgeous, even with the panicked look in her eyes. He sat back, took a bite and waited to hear what Kimmel had to say about his lover.

"And this girl . . . we gotta find out what's wrong with her. Cute though. We should get her for the show . . ."

Cute? She was more than cute.

"I hate it when people stare at me. I feel like a freak!" Hellboy turned to look at an unhappy Liz. He wasn't sure when she had emerged from her self-imposed bathroom exile but here she was, once more unhappy with the world. Her mood sapped the joy he was taking in the coverage.

With each step closer, his emotions shifted from pleasure to dread. He hated disappointing Liz and here he seemed to have gone and done it again.

"You had no right, Red. We decide together."

He was suddenly placed on the defensive, not something he liked. "Look —it was an accident."

She screwed up her face in disapproval. "Yeah, right."

Hellboy continued, "We came off great . . . TV is good for us . . ."

Looking back at the monitors, one news channel cut from Hellboy to Manning, who never looked good on TV. Sort of like Nixon, he decided. With twisted delight, he raised the volume on that particular screen.

"Yes, definitely: a gas . . . pocket . . ." It sounded even less authoritative or genuine on tape, he decided.

The screen cut from Manning to the commentator, who looked particularly grave, his forehead knit in concern, marring the carefully applied pancake makeup.

"The 'Gas Pocket' alibi was ridiculed by several political analysts and shows an absolute disregard . . ."

"Dear God . . ." Manning said, loud enough to fill the room and drown out both televisions.

He whirled about, pointing an accusatory finger in Hellboy's face. He probably deserved this. A little.

"You have *murdered* me," Manning cried out. "Murdered me. I asked you—no—no—I *begged* you to be . . ."

"Discreet," Abe said, once more finishing Manning's thought.

"Discreet. Thank you. But you, sir . . . You have crushed my political future—you have ridiculed me—you have crushed my hopes and—and you—you have—you have . . ." He paused, clearly struggling to contain himself. Idly, Hellboy wondered if Manning was going to strike him. Not that it would hurt him, but it might make Manning feel better and he was beginning to think he should let the fed have one shot. But only one.

"You have brought it unto yourself," Manning finally finished.

"What?"

Unhappy, Manning reached into his suit jacket and withdrew a paper where, just twenty-four hours earlier, a batch of Cubans had lain in wait. The paper looked official and a lot less appealing.

"You're going to get it. Washington is sending down a new B.P.R.D. agent."

Hellboy was displeased. He had only gotten used to Myers and then lost him. He figured it was just the team—him, Abe, Liz, and Manning. Who needed to break up the quartet with some new geek?

"What? A new guy?? Why??"

Ominously, Manning answered, "To look you over."

CHAPTER EIGHT

Nuada ceremoniously walked behind the chamberlain, flanked by the guards from the round house. They crossed several tracks, deeper into the yards and directly toward a machine shop. Nuala remained outside the procession, walking to the side, but matching her twin brother's pace. They exchanged glances and Nuada could tell she was disturbed. He had disappointed her and that pained him. He was also causing her some regret or personal pain, but every action could be justified. While they shared a connection unlike any other, they were not of one mind. As a result, she could not appreciate the confluence of events that informed his actions. He only hoped that once things unfolded she would understand and even accept the things that were to come.

His face wrinkled with disgust at the rats that scurried over the tracks and the torn papers that gently swirled in the cool, late-night breeze.

The moon was already beginning its descent and the prince knew the next hours would not be pleasant ones. Necessary ones, to be sure, but not ones he looked forward to. Still, they could not be avoided and with luck, the next time the council needed to meet, it would be in better circumstances.

The machine shop stank of oil and metal. For decades it had worked long hours as men repaired the locomotives, which belched coal smoke that fouled the air. As electricity replaced steam, the need for this shop dwindled and it was finally abandoned, an old friend allowed to wither and die from neglect. So wasteful. So much like mankind itself.

Tonight that would change.

Entering the shop, the guards split apart, opening a path for Nuada to walk alone. He strode with a purposeful gait, not breaking pace, and proceeded to the center. Since no man bothered to visit the building, it had been converted to an appropriate throne room, decorated with Elvish sigils, galleries and other trappings of court. Despite his exile, he had heard word when the throne left Europe and migrated to America, much like men. Too much like men—following in their footsteps.

Candles and lanterns illuminated the space, creating a large circle of light. Within it resided representatives of the Elvish families that comprised the council. All were old and had seen far better days, but responded to the summons nonetheless. A royal command was still powerful and could not be ignored.

At the far edge of the circle was his father, good King Balor. He was seated on a well-worn throne. Beside him was a slightly smaller throne chair which Nuala gracefully slid into. They sat side by side, comfortable with one another's company in a way that Nuada could only envy. He'd been gone too long, seen too much, and as a result, he and his father no longer could see the world in the same way.

Nuada's eyes focused on the crest Balor proudly wore on his chest. It nearly matched the one on the gown his sister wore and denoted their royalty.

Next, he studied his father, whom he had not seen in too long a span of years. Balor had not aged well, Nuada concluded.

The lines on his face showed the wear of time, the gray in his hair and eyebrows spoke of the centuries between visits. He seemed tired.

Balor's missing arm, lost in battle millennia ago, had been replaced with a wood and silver device that remained polished to a high sheen. The wooden contraption was placed carefully over his neck and shoulder, the joints around the elbow and wrist were all in filigreed silver, ending in a hand that was more decorative than functional. Carrying this added weight, strapped across his chest and back, no doubt added to the burden he bore as leader.

The doors to the vast chamber closed and Nuada neared the throne, Wink a few steps behind him. The chamberlain and the guards fanned out, taking their assigned places. Seated around the machine shop were rows of tiered brick-and-stone benches that housed the delegates from the Elvish families, summoned from around the world for this rare meeting.

All seemed ready but he knew he needed to be introduced to his father before he should speak. He could be patient for just a little while longer.

Finally, the chamberlain turned to King Balor and adjusted his voice to be heard. "His divine majesty, Prince Nuada, Silverlance."

Nuada bowed his head low then dropped to kneel before his father.

"Father."

"Why?!" the king cried in a voice filled with pain and anger. Its force surprised Nuada and he felt slapped even though they were merely words. "Why have you done this? Why?" The tremble in the voice made Nuada inwardly wince but he needed to endure it.

Done bowing, he rose, addressing his father, a determined look meeting his father's angry one. "To set us free," Nuada declared loudly. "All of us, Father."

The king shook his head in bewilderment. "You have broken a truce with mankind. A truce that has lasted for centuries."

"A truce based on shame."

That brought about murmurs from the assembled elves. None dared challenge Nuada or interrupt the exchange. Nuada seized on the break in stares and quickly glanced about the room, recognizing he had their full attention and was willing to discuss what the others would only say among themselves. He addressed the entire chamber, his voice filled with strength and conviction.

"The humans have forgotten the gods, destroyed the earth. And for what? Parking lots. Shopping malls. Greed has burned a hole in their chests that can never be filled. They will never have enough. I have walked this planet, watched them slaughter one another so they could build grander homes. I've seen the land raped, the resources wasted, and they are no better than they were when we made the agreement."

"What humans do is in their nature," Balor said, letting his aged voice carry. "To honor the agreement is in ours."

Nuada looked about him, seeing cobwebs on the periphery of the light, the cracked or missing windows. He saw dirt on the floor and tracks left behind by insects and vermin. It filled him with righteous rage.

"Look at this place. Where is the honor in this? Is this where you hold court? A derelict building. In the shadows—in their refuse? Where will you go next? The sewers with the trolls?"

Nuada then boldly stepped closer to his father, breaking tradition, and he made his case no longer to the assembled folk, but only to his sire. "Father," he pleaded with a firm voice. "You were once a proud warrior. When did you become their pet?"

The sting was clear as his father visibly shuddered and reached out to take Nuala's hand. She let his rough, thick fingers wrap around her own, and as he lowered his head, his sister appraised her twin and clearly wasn't happy with what she saw. That concerned him but would not sway him from the path he had begun years before.

"I have returned from exile to reclaim the land that is rightfully ours," Nuada said. "What sent me from court is past. This planet is at a tipping point—even the humans seem to have recognized that. What they do next will decide if this world is viable for all of us. I will not let them decide our fate."

He turned his gaze from his father and made his appeal to the others. The slowly nodding heads emboldened him and confirmed he was on the right path. "And for this we'll call the help of all the Children of the Earth. And they will answer: the good . . . the bad . . . and the worst."

To emphasize his point, he reached deep within the folds of his robes and withdrew the golden artifact liberated from the humans a day earlier. It caught the light and glittered for all to see. The reflection riveted his father's attention and seemed to break the heavy sadness that clouded his features. He recognized it, of course, and then those sad eyes smoldered. When he spoke, his words were filled once more with anger.

"Enough! You cannot be that mad."

Waving the portion of the crown in the air to aid his words, Nuada nodded in agreement. "Perhaps I am. Perhaps they made me so."

Finally, his sister spoke up and her eyes matched her father's. They burned in anger and disapproval. Once more they wounded Nuada but not mortally.

"And you think . . . that our green fields will grow out of all that blood? It may just be that our days are ended. Us . . . them . . . Sooner or later we will all fade."

Nuada responded with equal heat. "*Better to burn than fade away . . .*"

Balor looked at Nuada as a king would address any courtier. It was not a pleasant scene for any of the participants but it was necessary.

"For the last time, my son, I ask you . . . is this the path you wish to take?"

"It is. I am sorry, Father."

The room grew silent with anticipation. All eyes were on the king to see what he would do although all knew. Nuada knew, too. His father was predictable and had been steadfast in his dealings with mankind's world, allowing things to wither and die while he sat aging on his rotting throne.

"Then—you leave me no other choice. Death."

The last word resounded around the chamber and caused a fresh round of muttering. All asked one another if the king would really take the life of his son. Nuada knew the answer. His father would do anything, including having him killed, if it meant preserving the wretched status quo.

The butcher guards withdrew their swords, ready to honor their king's command.

Nuada ignored them and looked at his sister. She returned the gaze with a sad expression.

"And you, my sister, you are at peace with your king's verdict?"

Silently, she bowed her head in agreement.

"Very well then, death it is."

As if a signal had been sent, Nuada and Wink sprung into action. First, the prince moved to the guard holding his sword. The guard was taken by surprise and easily left his feet, allowing Nuada to regain possession of his prized weapon.

At the same moment, Wink easily caved in the head of a different guard, sending those nearest him scattering.

Cries of amazement rose from the assembled members of the council and many scattered away from the creature.

Nuada fought off two more guards, his sword slashing the air, its gleaming blade darkened with gore. The moves displayed his years of practice, a bloody ballet that easily cut down the king's guard.

His moves were so quick that the attackers were uncertain where to strike since he did not hold still, marring their aim. The dust he kicked up created clouds of dirt that blurred his motions to the spectators, none of which dared to leave the galleries. Leaves, dry and brittle, swirled around their ankles, crackling and snapping in addition to the sounds made from the blade slicing through armor. Rarely was there the sound of metal on metal, as Nuada's aim was true. He parried, thrust and moved on.

When several of the guards finally began to work in unison, Nuada surprised them by leaping high over their heads and grabbing on to a long-forgotten canvas water hose, using it as a rope and swinging away from their combined might. Their jaws gaped as he freely flew over their heads.

Nuada further surprised them by grabbing a second hose and swinging further away, balancing off a wall and then springing into the air, his sword at the ready, into a cluster of guards, caught totally unawares. An arm flew into the first row of the nearest gallery, a fountain of dark blood trailing behind it. A sword fell to the ground with a loud clang.

He finally faced off against a guard who seemed to know what he was doing and blocked a thrust from the prince. A sly smile crossed his face, and Nuada was pleased to see at least one of the guards was well trained. He privately wept at how the standards for his father's guard had deteriorated. The guard parried a swing then ducked under the prince's sword as it swung in the opposite direction. He landed a solid blow to the prince's chest, actually staggering him backward.

Enough play time, he mused, and sprang from his heels and grabbed a different hose, rising into the air, avoiding a second punch. Nuada then let the hose carry him above the fray and once more, his powerful legs braced against the wall as he studied the butcher guard. The guard snarled, drool pooling in one corner of his mouth, eager to continue the fight.

Nuada accommodated him by pushing away from the wall, swinging directly at the guard, his sword at the ready. The guard braced himself, feet spread apart, poised for the attack.

A flick of his wrist and the sword elongated to become a lance, then a hurtling weapon, cutting the distance between them in mere seconds. It landed deep in the guard's chest, catching him by surprise, eyes staring in wonder at the bubbling blood springing from the mortal wound. He then toppled backward, the force of the blow finally forcing him to move.

The prince lightly touched down while none of the other guards dared approach him, even unarmed. He bent low to retrieve his weapon and as he withdrew it from the now-dead guard, Nuada heard the rustle of leather and knew a new attack was imminent.

The lance free, it whirled in an arc to his right and sliced right into the midsection of the attacker, gutting him sight unseen.

His eyes darted around the room and saw that Wink had held back, allowing his master the honor of dispatching the guard. The two exchanged glances and a silent nod passed between them.

Wink finally moved, flanking Nuada's rear as the prince, now splattered in blood, guts, and dust, his fine robes ruined, approached the throne. Balor did not move, nor did his sister. Hatred smoldered in the former's aged eyes, sending the prince into a fresh rage.

Rushing the short stairs to the throne, Nuada neatly stabbed his father with the sword, killing him with the blow.

"I always loved you, Father."

Nuada would never know if his final words penetrated the dying monarch's mind, registering at all. It didn't matter, really. The die was cast and the world of creatures was now committed to his course of action.

Balor began to turn from flesh to ash and finally the prince could look no longer. The ash statue of what had been his father collapsed into a pile of dust. The passing of a king went unheralded. An age ended.

Nuala sat in stunned silence, tears freely falling over her cheeks. She refused to meet her brother's eyes.

The prince reached forward, digging his hand into the thick pile of ashes, digging within the clothes his father had worn. The wooden and silver artificial-arm apparatus was grimy, and clattered to the ground, finally free of its host. Nuada's arm rooted around and finally withdrew, clutching the second piece of the crescent crown. Slowly, he studied it, admiring its runes. Then, he withdrew the fragment he had obtained and held them near one another. With a theatric flare, he moved them closer very slowly, letting the pieces become aware of each other. As they touched, bits and pieces of the ends fused, connections completed, and within seconds, the two pieces were fused together, the seam undetectable.

Two thirds were now reunited and Nuada was pleased.

One third retrieved from an unwitting mankind, one from the Children of the Earth. One third remained in his people's possession and it too needed to be obtained.

He raised it high, allowing the stunned and still silent council to see it, letting them gaze on something most only knew from legends and bedtime stories. Stepping forward, milking the moment, he waved it about, making certain all got a glimpse of his treasure.

"Hear me, all!" he cried out. No one challenged him, none wishing to join Balor and the butcher guards in oblivion. They watched and listened, their expressions a mix of horror and sadness, and one or two showed anticipation. They were not all sheep—some would listen and heed his words. "I bring forth a message of war. And to this council that message is brief and clear: you may join us or die here—now. All of those against it, make it known."

He looked from gallery to gallery, and saw scarred, silent faces. Then, one by one, they bowed their heads in acquiescence. Within moments, the assembled leaders of the Elvish world had silently pledged their loyalty to Nuada. They all accepted his call to war.

He would not be denied.

"I see you are as brave as always," the contempt dripped from his lips. They were sheep, too old and too frightened to do anything but follow him.

Nuada began to turn back to the dais, ready to make this a family affair.

"And now, my sister . . ."

But her chair was empty. His eyes quickly scanned the vicinity but she was gone.

Where on earth could she flee to now?

He did not see her, deep in the shadows behind the thrones, near a staircase that was crumbling from neglect. Nuala moved noiselessly. From a compartment in the wide belt encircling her own silken robes, she removed the final third of the crescent, rubbing it back and forth in her hands.

Had her brother realized it was so near, even her life would have been threatened.

She slipped out a back way.

CHAPTER NINE

The B.P.R.D. exterior was in harmony with its surround-ings. Unobtrusive stone and brick mixed in among the trees. On the inside, though, things were quite different. Through the years, constant upgrades saw to it the facility was state of the art, capable of holding whatever paranormal beastie was brought to its confines. No expense, it seemed, was spared when it came to making certain visitors were met with shock and awe at the scope and sheer power the head-quarters projected.

Marble and chrome, recessed lighting, panels hiding scanners and security devices surrounded the quartet as they stood waiting for their new arrival. Liz had her hands in her pockets, her shoulders slumped, and Manning couldn't begin to imagine what was bugging her this morning. The sun was out, they still had their jobs, and things were going to turn around. Everything pointed to the newest member of the team being just what he needed to bring Hellboy to heel. If anyone was happy with the day, it was Thomas Manning.

Abe and Hellboy talked among themselves, ignoring Manning, which was fine. He was used to it since neither re-ally liked change all that much.

"We don't need this guy," Hellboy said to Abe.

Manning walked over, keeping out of reach just in case. "I think we do," he asserted. "Evidently, this guy's quite the big shot in Washington."

"What's his name?" As expected, Hellboy impulsively reached out, trying to grab the manila personnel file in Manning's hand. It was like keeping candy away from a child, Manning thought. He knew Hellboy's extended lifespan meant he was in demon adolescence, but his actions spoke of a ten-year-old. So Manning treated him as such.

Confirming his memory, he glanced at the folder and then announced: "Johann Krauss."

"Sounds German."

Manning kept the file open, hoping to get some pertinent details settled in Hellboy's porous brain. "Top man in ecto . . ." He struggled with the pronunciation, until Abe smoothly filled in the gap.

"Ectoplasmic."

Manning rolled ahead while he had Hellboy's attention. ". . . research. Comes highly recommended by our European liaison."

A light winked to life and Manning knew it was to be followed by an alarm. The doors were about to open and their new leader would emerge. Whatever else he wanted to impart to his charges would have to wait.

He was looking forward to some order. To someone taking charge of Hellboy and reining him in. Lord knows, he had tried. Practically rubbing his hands with glee, Manning beamed.

"Liaison. Love that word. Don't you? So hoity toity."

"Here he is," Liz said, the first words she had uttered all day it seemed. She remained somewhat distracted but that was going to be Krauss's concern now.

"I don't like Germans," Hellboy rumbled.

Manning quickly checked the file to see if he might be Austrian instead; anything to keep Hellboy open minded.

"Germans make me nervous."

"No fingerprints," Manning read from the file and the words caught Abe's interest. "No photo. But the dossier says, and I translate, that . . . he has . . . a nice, open face . . ."

At that, the elevator doors smoothly slid apart revealing six B.P.R.D. agents in dark suits and sunglasses looking like so many Men in Black. In their center, though, was someone most definitely not a cookie-cutter agent. Manning's eyes bulged at the sight of the six-foot-tall figure, clad entirely in a thick canvas containment suit, crisscrossed with tubes and bristling with taps. There were leather pieces at the joints and the entire portion from the shoulders up was in brown leather, culminating in a clear helmet.

Where a smiling face should have been was a swirling gas that only vaguely suggested a human head. And only then if you squinted.

Johann Krauss strode forward and stood there, knowing full well he was being studied. Manning would have expected it if their roles had been reversed which, thank God, they were not.

". . . Oh my God . . ." he said and then shut his mouth, totally embarrassed his thoughts had been audible.

Krauss ignored Manning and even Hellboy, making a bee-line for Liz, who appraised him without flinching. He stopped a short distance from her and took her right hand in his gloved one. He then bowed deeply, the very model of an eastern European soldier.

"My outward appearance might be shocking," the voice emitted from a speaker secreted within the suit said. It was slightly accented, once more indicating his origins. Surprisingly, it was warm and friendly, not at all mechanically produced. Just what was Krauss?

"I know," he said, still holding Liz's hand. "But within the confines of this containment suit beats the heart of an Austrian gentleman. Johann Krauss, at your service." Austrian, thank goodness. He wasn't a straight German; there was still a chance for Hellboy to like him.

"I like him," Abe happily told Manning. Well, that was to be expected.

Hellboy merely studied him, noncommittal.

In a medical bay unlike anything else controlled by the federal government, the team reassembled. Krauss ordered an agent to have his belongings stowed in his quarters. He'd attend to them later but first came work and the matter at hand was understanding what had happened days earlier.

As they moved from the lobby to the medical center, Manning made a round of introductions and the responses went as expected. Abe was friendly and followed Emily Post to a T. Liz was quiet and answered questions when asked but offered nothing. Manning was, of course, the model of a modern politician. Hellboy checked the containment suit for oily spots after Krauss and Manning had shaken hands.

Krauss was another freak and seemed totally comfortable with the group, which made for a faster adjustment than poor Myers. And these days, now that the freaks were out, he'd remain comfortable with the team. Still, Hellboy wondered how a guy like that had turned into living gas—more to the point, how had he worked with the government and avoided being assigned to the B.P.R.D. before now. He must have been valuable and at that, Hellboy felt a pang of jealously. After all, he used to be the golden—or crimson—boy.

The group was clustered around an examination table, a variety of monitors whirring and beeping, none of which told Hellboy a damned thing. A giant lighted magnifying glass on a swivel arm was adjusted over the specimen atop the tissue-paper covering. It was just one of the tooth fairies; dozens had been taken from the auction house while the rest were incinerated by the Bureau. Dead, it seemed cute once more, except for the tears in its skin revealing orange and red organs. Krauss was positioning the magnifier for a closer look.

Their new leader clicked a nonexistent tongue in sympathy as he used a probe to look underneath what was probably a lung.

"Look at that. Poor things, bought and sold on the black market. Crammed into cargo containers, smuggled, abused, held captive."

As Krauss fussed over the fairy corpse, Abe was studying a collection of prints, taken by other agents in the wake of the attack. Interestingly, the iron containers that housed the tooth fairies remained intact. Whatever metal they were made from was clearly stronger than most commercial-grade stuff. Abe was inspecting the royal seal on the box, something that seemed familiar to Hellboy. He'd seen it before, long ago, but he couldn't conjure up the exact details. In fact, it gnawed at him a bit and that didn't help his mood.

Liz remained aloof. Manning remained a pompous jerk. Now he had Krauss to deal with.

Manning leaned over Krauss's shoulder, the suck-up, and looked at the tiny, charred body. He seemed more interested in watching how Krauss worked than the actual subject on the table.

"He has very expressive hands," Manning said in an aside to Abe.

Thankfully, the fish-man ignored the comment and remained focused on the picture. Finally, he said, "The seal on the box worries me also."

Krauss immediately raised his bubble head and looked in Abe's direction.

"Very good. I noticed that," he said, a teacher proud of his new student.

"A royal emblem."

"Very, very, very good." Hellboy rolled his eyes. That condescending tone was going to drive him nuts.

"From the Bethmoora clan—the Sons of the Earth," Abe suggested.

Sons of the Earth, okay, that sounded familiar. What did he know about them, Hellboy mused.

"Your file says you are the brains of the operation. And I must admit, I am impressed."

Abe would have blushed if he didn't have scaly blue skin. Heck, he might have been blushing and they couldn't tell. Finally, someone appreciated that big brain of his and there'd be an intellectual equal for him to talk with. There hadn't been one of those in a while.

Not since Broom passed away.

"And in my file—you'll see, Mr. Krauss—that I've worked closely with Abe in his training," Manning hastily added, clearly seeking credit.

Hellboy let out a sound that was both derisive and filled with disgust.

Manning sneered at him, out of Krauss's presumed field of vision.

"Let's see what our little friend here can remember, shall we?" The cheerful tone was already grating to Hellboy. This boss wasn't going to work.

"Memory gets pretty sketchy when you burn to death," Hellboy said. He then nudged Abe and added, "But maybe St. Malachy can help."

Hellboy reached into a pocket and withdrew the amulet with the saint's image on it.

Krauss stared at it and then shook his head.

"No amulets, *meinen Herren*."

With that, Krauss adjusted one of the myriad valves at the tips of his gloved fingers and reached toward the dead fairy. A white-gray gas slowly curled from the valve and snaked forward, touching the shrunken body on the table.

Abe was watching in fascination and finally spoke up. "Teleplasty?"

"Correct, Agent Sapien." Hellboy wondered when this guy was going to start handing out gold stars.

"Plastic? He uses plastic? Very swanky," Manning added because he felt obligated to contribute to the conversation, even when he had absolutely nothing of note to contribute. Why couldn't he take lessons from Liz, who watched and absorbed and contributed only when there was something useful, or wonderfully snarky, to add.

Turning to Manning, Abe said in a teacher's tone that seemed identical to Krauss's, "Teleplasty, by which an ectoplasmic medium can inhabit inanimate things: organic, mechanical . . ."

The lecture was interrupted by Krauss, who had ignored the others and was concentrating entirely on the creature. "Ah, good. I have control of its limbic system."

Hellboy studied the creature, which, defying logic, was once more breathing. The chest rose and fell with shallow breaths so now he knew exactly what Abe was babbling about. Krauss placed the zombie fairy in the palm of his hand and watched it. The thing sat up and stared at Hellboy; recognizing him, it bared its teeth and hissed at him.

"What?" he demanded of the thing. "You chewed off the top of my tail. Yes, you—you little . . ."

The not-so-dead fairy chattered on in a high-pitched tone, cutting him off with nonsense sounds. Krauss was listening to it with an intensity which mystified Hellboy.

Krauss stopped listening and offered a translation. "It says you are rude, brutish, and not too bright."

"Wow," came a voice and Hellboy looked over to see that Liz finally chose to speak up and sure enough, she was feeling snarky.

Before he could say something to her, the thing continued to yammer away in Fairy.

"It seems our little friend here remembers market sounds and voices. A very peculiar tongue, spoken in the last place where his cage was opened."

Krauss considered a word and finally translated it to his satisfaction and added, "Troll language."

"The Troll Market? C'mon . . ."

The vigorous nodding from the fairy interrupted Liz's comments. Hellboy knew of the Troll Market; heck, most B.P.R.D. agents came across references to it at some point or another. No one, not even long-lived Abe, had ever been to it. They couldn't find it despite various attempts over the years.

Broom had told him about it on more than one occasion and it sounded like a fascinating cross between the Union Square Farmer's Market and the set from Tod Browning's *Freaks*.

"No one's ever found it," she continued, confirming Hellboy's knowledge.

" 'Cause it doesn't exist," he added to bolster her claim. She ignored him.

The tooth zombie seemed to disagree and worked itself up into a state, chattering on until it abruptly slowed. It appeared to fade in color and clearly, whatever Krauss could do was only temporary.

"Mr. Krauss," Manning said. "Uh, Dr. Krauss, sir. Our little informant there—he doesn't look too good."

Well, duh. Anyone could see it was failing as the cheekbones grew hollow and then it collapsed in a heap, still in Krauss's palm.

"I'm with you, pal," Hellboy said to the once-more-dead fairy. "He has the same effect on me."

The ectoplasm that had enlivened the body seeped out and returned to the containment suit, reuniting with the rest of Krauss. It was eerie to watch, Hellboy decided.

Once the valves were resealed, Krauss addressed his team in a commanding voice. "So. There—now we have a lead. Trolls dwell under bridges."

"You're a genius," Hellboy said.

Ignoring him, Krauss continued. "And Vladimir Vanya, nineteenth-century occult historian, places the Troll Market directly under the east end of the Brooklyn Bridge."

Hellboy and the others all nodded in agreement. "We looked already."

Krauss, though, shook his bubble head. "No, no . . . not with me, Agent. Not with me. We're moving in."

CHAPTER TEN

Brooklyn Bridge
9:00 P.M.

The Brooklyn Bridge was a fabled construction in engineering circles. The span was nearly six thousand feet and took thirteen years to build. When it opened in 1883, it spelled the end of Brooklyn's independence, going from the fourth-largest city in America to a borough of New York. Just building it spawned countless stories and since then it had become a cultural landmark.

Crossing over from Manhattan, the B.P.R.D.'s no-longer-discreet garbage truck and several other vehicles arrived on the eastern side of the bridge. They parked near the base of the bridge, a stench wafting over them from the East River. The air was also filled with the pungent odors coming from a nearby meat packing plant which was clearly still at work.

It was dark and a haze filled the air, blurring the lights from nearby apartment buildings and still-open businesses. Alcoholics and homeless people congregated near tall cans that burned garbage to generate heat and light. Most huddled around it to combat the chill night air. None paid them any attention.

While Hellboy relished the media exposure, he didn't need them interrupting the work that needed doing. He was determined to still be a good agent, just one that wasn't skulking about when he needed to stomp out evil.

He rubbed his coat sleeve over a smudge on the Samaritan, out and ready, just in case. Right now, he'd like to use it on the agent leading the team toward the granite base of the bridge.

" 'Not with me, Agent'? What an ego!"

"I like him," Abe said quietly. He stopped walking and knelt down beside Krauss. They were carefully opening a wooden, square crate that was stenciled with black letters and numbers. Abe gripped the lid and read from the side panel.

"Lot 336. The Smithsonian Institute. Could it be?"

"Yes," Krauss said, sharing the fish-man's enthusiasm. "Three pairs."

"Oh, my God," Abe exclaimed with an enthusiasm Hellboy hadn't heard in ages. "The Schufftein glasses. How . . . ?"

"I made a few phone calls," Krauss replied, sounding like it was the kind of thing he did all the time.

While the two were geeking out over the toys, Hellboy found himself alone with Liz for what felt like the first time in days. Looking for something to talk about other than their issues, he asked, "What did you think of Mr. Know-It-All?"

"Too early to tell."

And then she was handed a pair of the glasses, a set of copper-and-glass goggles that were covered with complicated gears and rods. The telescoping, nearly foot-long lenses gyrated as if alive, but some inner engine must have powered them. They looked downright bizarre on her and he had no idea what they allowed her to see.

She gazed around the area, from Hellboy to the bridge and to the collection of addicts and winos nearby. "They must really like this guy in Washington," she marveled. "We've been trying to get these for years."

"I think he's full of himself,"

With the glasses still on, Liz eyed him closely.

"Look, Red . . . I think he knows who he is and what he wants. And that rubs you the wrong way." She then wandered away from him, leaving him bewildered by her, more so than usual.

"What's that supposed to mean?"

Abe, as usual, came to the rescue, leaning in close and speaking softly, so Krauss wouldn't hear the exchange. "He's sure of himself and I think maybe . . . you feel threatened."

The amphibian strolled after Liz, leaving Hellboy to ponder those words by himself.

10:30 P.M.

He took his assigned position on the rooftop of a movie theater, the marquee lights keeping people from easily seeing him. Not that there were many moviegoers at this hour, but it's where Krauss wanted him.

Settling in for what was sure to be a fruitless night, he ripped open a bag of Cheetos and muttered to himself, "Threatened?! Ah! Me? Threatened?"

Stuffing a handful of the bright orange snacks into his mouth, he leaned over the edge of the rooftop, which afforded him a clear view of the garbage truck. Standing in front of it were Liz and Manning.

He had rarely felt more isolated from his true love.

He ate more Cheetos.

Manning was staring at Liz's goggles and it made her uncomfortable even though she had the rare artifact to hide behind.

She just disliked being stared at under any circumstances. He should have known better but Manning was particularly artless, which was bad for a politician.

"What do these things do?"

"Fairy folk and trolls generate a cloaking aura called 'glamour.' In 1878, Emil Schufftein designed and built four crystal diopters that penetrate that effect and allow the wearer to see . . ."

She paused, staring at herself in the truck's side-view mirror.

"To see things the way they really are," she finished.

Up on the roof, Abe and Krauss joined Hellboy, who was keeping a noisy vigil. Orange dust littered Hellboy's coat. Through the glasses he wore over his goggles, Abe thought it added an unusual glow.

As Abe adjusted and practiced with the various configurations of lenses and prisms, Krauss walked back and forth, a general ready to give his troop marching orders.

"We will enter the market and look for any sign of this seal—find out who sold those creatures to the perpetrator. We will do this by the book. You will follow my orders. Any questions?"

Hellboy raised a red and orange hand.

"Yes?" He seemed surprised to be asked anything at all and Abe knew something superfluous was coming.

"Mr. Kraut, sir?"

"Krauss, Agent. With a double S." Abe winced, unnoticed.

"S.S.," Hellboy repeated, then stuffed another handful of Cheetos in his mouth before continuing. "Mmh. Look—you're new here, so you wouldn't know, but, headgear or no headgear, this is a waste of time."

Now it was Krauss's turn to repeat a phrase. "A waste of time?"

"Colossal."

"Protest noted," Strauss said dismissively. "Thank you, Agent."

"And those gizmos?" Krauss nodded for him to continue. As Hellboy babbled, Abe adjusted his glasses and studied Hellboy. He pierced the coat and clothes, could see past the red-hued epidermis and actually got a close-hand look at his friend's organs and skeletal structure. The partially digested orange clump of Cheetos in his stomach gave him a wave of nausea.

"How do you know if they work?"

Any reply was thankfully interrupted by Liz's voice coming over their earpieces. "*I have a suspect,*" she announced.

"Give me a vector, Agent Sherman. A vector." To Abe, Krauss sounded anxious, ready for action, so maybe he was more like Hellboy than he had first thought. There was definitely more to him than just a kindred spirit.

"'What's the vector, Victor?' I love that stuff," Hellboy said, earning him what appeared to be an uncomprehending look from Krauss. Abe stifled a chuckle.

"*B-12, sir, the alley. Northbound.*"

"Track the target. We're coming down."

Liz snapped off the channel and checked the map on the wall. It was festooned with pins and crisscrossed with lines chopping Brooklyn into a grid that could be understood by any agent.

Manning was studying the monitor. He seemed not to understand why a bag lady had caught her attention. Good as he was with managing the media and Washington, Manning just didn't have the awareness to be an effective field agent. He insisted on coming along to impress the new boss, Krauss. As long as he wasn't in the way, she didn't particularly care.

"Keep an eye on her. I'll be right back."

He thumbed the screen, as the old woman pushed her requisite shopping cart, although this one was filled with cats as opposed to all her worldly possessions. Then again, maybe it was.

"That little old lady? Oh, please, she's just as sweet as she can . . ."

Liz interrupted him, handing him the third pair of special glasses. She helped adjust them on his ears and then directed him at the screen once more. Once he had stared at it, she too looked at the screen. Sure enough, the old woman's appearance was pierced and within the glamour was an ugly, muscle-bound troll; nothing sweet about that.

"A fragglewump," she explained. "Scottish troll. Very ugly."

Manning rubbed a hand across his now-sweaty scalp. "Oh, dear lord. What about the kittens?"

"She feeds on them."

Grabbing a cage containing a sleeping canary, she exited the truck and prepared to join the others as instructed. She was good at following orders, bringing a semblance of structure to her life. As she closed the door, she heard Manning complain.

"That thing—it's a 'she'?"

As Liz crossed the street to join the others, Hellboy watched her. The distance between them had never felt greater and he was damned if he knew what was really troubling her. Sure, the mess had to be a part of it, but it was clear there was another issue on her mind. He just wasn't up for guessing. There were too many options.

Once she arrived, they headed out in a silent pack, trailing the oblivious bag lady—or fragglewump, as Krauss was all too happy to explain—as she headed away from the streets and toward the meat market. She looked around once, shushed a cat to be still, and then entered the worn building. It was humming with power, but clearly hadn't been used to properly pack meat in ages. Cobwebs that would have driven a health inspector nuts were just the beginning of the offenses to be cataloged.

From a distance, they watched her walk to the rear of the building and, checking over her shoulder in the gloom, enter the mammoth walk-in refrigerator.

Liz leaned over and handed Hellboy the cage, the closest they'd been in some time. It lasted for seconds.

"You may need this."

"Good thinking!" he told her.

Krauss stared at the cage in wonderment, or Hellboy supposed it was wonderment. After all, a glass bowl full of gas made it hard to understand the man's body language. Still, he liked that Mr. Know-It-All didn't, well, know it all.

"Agent . . . what is that?"

She gave him one of her patented withering looks and Hellboy was pleased it was directed at someone other than himself for a change.

"Trolls fear canaries," she said, approximating the same tone he used when explaining things he felt others should already know.

"Oh. Nursery rhymes. You all believe in nursery rhymes." He was mocking them and Hellboy felt his blood begin to boil. He flexed his free hand open and closed to avoid striking his fellow agent.

"Sometimes to know the beat you've gotta be on the beat," she added flippantly. Then, she walked away, leaving Hellboy to do his thing.

Watching her move off, admiring her gait, Hellboy said to no one in particular, "I love her."

Hellboy neared the still-open refrigerator and could feel the cooler air drift his way. It was cooler than the night air, he noted, and imagined how a troll would enjoy the drop in temperature. Less than he did, that was for sure.

Her movements were obvious thanks to the still-functioning light bulbs, although they were of low wattage and several flickered, causing the rows of meat hooks to cast odd shadows against the stained and grimy walls. She then slowed her passage and came to a stop, arousing his curiosity. The sweet-looking woman reached into the cage that kept her cats safely in her basket. A young and particularly adorable black-and-tan kitten meowed unhappily as she lifted it by the scruff of the neck.

She petted it a few times to calm it down and it nestled in her arms. Her look was not of an owner content with its pet but more of a predator about to pounce.

"She's gonna eat a cat," he said to Krauss.

The agent was unmoved by the tension in Hellboy's voice or the action they were about to witness. "Shh—you'll alert her to our presence."

"But she's gonna eat it," he complained.

Refusing to comment further, Krauss gave both Hellboy and Abe a rough shove, away from their exposed positions and further behind the haphazardly stacked pile of packing crates.

Hellboy complied, understanding the urgency involved. Once he had crouched down, he did manage to sneak a peek at the lady through a gap between two of the large, splintered crates.

She was sniffing the air, clearly on the alert from the noise they had all just made. The kitten was arching its back, hair standing on end, requiring her to calm it down once more. Hellboy leaned forward for a better glimpse but just then he felt Krauss loom over him.

"You will follow my orders . . . and stay put until we can move in safely . . . do you understand?" he whispered in a harsh voice that was clearly lowered by the speaker affixed to the containment suit.

Hellboy was more fascinated by the old woman opening her mouth wide, wider, and wider still. He fairly gaped at the sight, unaware a person could stretch their mouth so wide—until he recalled she was anything but human.

"I'm talking to you, Agent," Krauss said with emphasis, almost hissing. "Do you understand? You are directly under my command—you have to follow . . ."

"Screw this." Hellboy had had enough of being ordered around by someone who had just showed up and hadn't bothered to get the lay of the land or understand the men under his command. Well, men and woman. He also disliked the idea of an innocent kitten becoming anyone's midnight buffet. He shrugged off Krauss's hand, passed the cage to a startled Abe, then rose; both hands wrapped around the Samaritan.

"No—wait!"

Hellboy ignored Krauss. Emerging from behind the crates, he walked across the street, casually, and called out, "Hey Luceee . . . I'm home!"

The woman looked up and her mouth instantly snapped back to human proportions and curled in a kindly smile. The kitten, unaware of its reprieve, continued to purr in her hands.

"Yes, m'dearie . . . what is it?"

Since he was wearing the glasses, all it took was a minute adjustment and he saw her for what she was, a snarling, drooling, ravenous troll. Amazing how good the glamour was, he noted. As Hellboy approached, she lowered the kitten, placing it freely atop the cage containing the rest of her larder.

"Give it up, Nasty," he told her. Tapping a red finger against the Schufftein goggles, he added, "We can see you."

The placid expression on the woman's face changed in an instant, eyes widening, the smile going from benign to fixed and grim. It appeared to shimmer a little, too. Maybe it was the lenses.

"Ye sssssee me? Ye sssssee me? How . . . how do ye sssssee me?" The voice began to sound different, more grating, deepening in tone. There was also a note of panic, which pleased him very much.

"We are looking for the entrance to the Troll Market. Any clues?"

She gaped at him, then her lips curled into a snarl while her eyes narrowed. The woman no longer looked sweet, nor did it appear she was going to give up her secrets easily. He hoped there'd be a fight; he felt like hitting something and suspected hitting Krauss would not go over well. Hitting a troll, though, that was probably permitted.

"Come any closer and I'll rip yer heart out," she warned him. Her look was one intended to menace and scare him off. Clearly, she had no idea who she was dealing with.

"Abe," he called over his shoulder, "let's get old school. Hand me the bird."

Abe stepped out from behind the crates, raising the hand holding the canary in the cage. Once she had locked her eyes on it, her expression shifted again, to one of outright panic. Krauss, behind Abe, stood still and no doubt wasn't enjoying the moment at all. Hellboy was savoring this since they so rarely had the upper hand at the outset of a case.

"Seeyach!! A canary!"

Hellboy shrugged at her, ignoring the inhuman hisses coming from her. "What? You're afraid of this li'l guy? Really? Who would know?" He then took the cage from Abe and thrust it toward the old woman, or troll, or whatever she pretended to be.

"Nooooo! Nooooo! I take you there!!"

An arthritic finger pointed to a dented, partly rusted sign that clearly was created back in the 1950s. On it in faded colors were the words, "Happy Cows Mean Tasty Beef."

Hellboy nodded with approval and walked past her, ignoring her snarls as the cage got a little too close, and he examined the large tin sign. He pulled it down and was rewarded with a ramp leading below the ground. The air was less cool from below, the pathway dark and forbidding.

Pretty much as he had expected, to be honest.

Abe, who had been watching from a discreet distance, signaled Krauss to come join them. Hellboy knew better than to go into the unknown without reinforcements. Manning and the German—no, Austrian—may have thought him a lunkhead, but he was anything but. As he waited, he made certain the oversized pistol was loaded and patted a pocket filled with additional ammunition. Even so, he suspected if it really came to a firefight, they would be seriously outnumbered.

Finally, he arrived and they surrounded the unhappy bag lady. He knew they were keeping her from dinner, but worse, she had also revealed what was one of her world's most closely guarded secrets. Even as a kid, he had heard stories from Broom about the market and its wonders—and dangers. The idea that things like the tooth fairies could be bought and sold there displeased Hellboy and he would have been happy shutting it down, closing the book on the legend. A part of him was also curious to see what it looked like, who shopped there, and what else might be for sale. The tug of curiosity was powerful and had gotten him into trouble in the past but tonight he was prepared.

Nothing would go wrong. This was a reconnaissance mission, so if they merely looked around, and didn't try to shut it down—this visit—then maybe, just maybe, things would go smoothly.

Yeah, right.

Abe used a flashlight to illuminate the clearly rough-hewn tunnel, formed from unfinished bedrock. The walls were unmarked and flickering fluorescent lights every few yards provided the only illumination. That meant electricity ran to the market, new information for them to digest.

With a wave of his hand, Hellboy indicated the old lady should lead the way into the tunnel. As she began to move, he reached over and took the kitten from her hands, and it shifted in his hand, seeking a comfortable perch. Hellboy sadly thought of Clump, long gone now, as he stroked the top of the kitten's head. It mewled once and then settled in place.

The legends of the trolls, the royal seal, and now thoughts of Clump were all swirling in his mind, dredging up memories long unvisited. He was determined to figure out why it all felt so familiar.

She snarled once, then walked past him, pointedly not looking at the cage, and headed into the dimly lit tunnel.

Onward they followed, all curious to see what was at the other end.

CHAPTER ELEVEN

Hellboy lost track of how long they'd been walking down the ramp, through the dank, mildewy tunnel. He also didn't stop to examine what was making the scraping noises on the ground since he doubted they posed a threat. The old lady continued walking slowly, but steadily, and the occasional mewling from the cats reminded them that they were far from alone. Still, it *felt* creepy and he continued to caress the Samaritan, poised and ready to fire.

Neither Abe nor Krauss said a word as they followed, which was fine with Hellboy. Even the kitten, asleep in his right hand, remained silent. It allowed him to concentrate, remain alert, and not get distracted with the two of them discussing paranormal string theory or whatever interested them now. The lights were strung further and further apart with more pools of utter darkness between them. As a result, he trusted the amazing penetrating ability of the goggles he wore, even though they were tight and unwieldy given their extended lenses. The troll/bag lady remained right in his field of vision and that meant all was well.

Finally, the tunnel ended. The edges of the tunnel walls curved slightly outward, opening up the space and finally wrapping around the rock that comprised the end of their path. The base of the tunnel was a huge storage area with steel containers stacked on either side of the door. Set well into the bedrock was a mammoth metallic door with latches, locks, and doodads all over the place. He doubted there was a key somewhere under all those cats in her cart. The woman stopped and made no effort to open the door or help them in any way, which was to be expected.

Hellboy let out a low whistle and said, "That's some door."

Abe stood beside him and studied the locking mechanism, the antique goggles lifted high on his forehead.

"Not good," he concluded. "With this number of symbols on the lock we'll be here for days."

"Not necessarily," Krauss began. "I can . . ."

In no mood for a lecture or a show-and-tell presentation, Hellboy turned to the old lady and ordered, "Open it, Luceee."

The bag lady stood her ground, arms folded defiantly. "I will *not*."

Krauss looked ready to try deciphering the lock and once more a wave of impatience flooded Hellboy. Standing around in this tunnel was not how he wanted to spend the next few days as his new colleague tried to show his superiority.

"I can handle . . ." Krauss started to say but was once more cut off by Hellboy, who hefted the canary cage in the old woman's line of sight.

"Pretty please." He even smiled at the disguised troll as he held up the canary, now free of its cage.

"Eyaaagh!!"

That did it and through the goggles, Hellboy watched the troll snarl and hiss, the features twisted in disgust and hatred.

"Do as ye may, Demon, release the yellow beast," the troll intoned. "It can have its way with me, but the market—it's the last place we have left. I won't give you the combination."

Hellboy seemed to ponder that for a moment and then asked, "You're absolutely sure of that?"

"Kill me and tear me eyes and rip me insides and me legs and me tongue—but I will *never* open that door."

Krauss once more made for the combination lock and again Hellboy impeded his path. This time, he handed the kitten to Abe, who gently accepted the burden.

"All right then."

With that, he reared back and delivered a powerful punch with his right hand that packed enough force to send the troll flying across the tunnel and into a stack of containers. Where human skin and bone would have been shredded by the impact, the troll's tougher hide withstood the blow and actually dented the metallic boxes. The troll slumped to the ground in a daze.

Krauss rushed forward, bending low to study the limp form. "Is that your 'investigative' technique?!" He most certainly didn't sound happy, not that Hellboy cared.

"She said never," he replied defensively.

"It's appalling." Oh yeah, Krauss was most certainly displeased. Time to earn brownie points.

"Really? What about this?" He raised his gun and fired off multiple rounds, each one finding its target, the elaborate lock. Metal flew apart, sparks flared, and the sound echoed throughout the tunnel.

And the door remained closed.

"*Mein Gott*," Krauss said when the final echo faded. He stepped between Hellboy, who stood sheepishly off to the side and faced the door. "Are you done? Step aside. You are a disgrace."

The suited man stood before the lock and adjusted the valves at the tip of each hand. Once more, a portion of his ectoplasmic essence seeped out and filled the spaces in and around the lock.

The lock tumblers began to spin about, symbols and numbers revolving until one by one, each space was filled with a final digit. When the last tumbler fell into place, a sound indicated the locks were being withdrawn. Gears spun and it was clear the entrance was about to open.

Hellboy had to give their new leader props for having the ability to do that. Now, if Krauss had only done that earlier, he wouldn't have wasted his ammunition.

As the door swung open as part of the unlocking process, a proud Krauss stepped ahead of them and gestured within.

"Gentlemen, welcome to the Troll Market."

Before Hellboy could take a step, the kitten leapt from Abe's hands and ran ahead of them, even more eager to explore the smells, sights, and sounds that awaited them. The whimpering troll forgotten, they followed the cat into the marketplace.

Hellboy wasn't sure what to expect as visions of Diagon Alley, Oz, and Cynosure danced in his mind. What he saw, instead, was far from those fanciful images. The Troll Market had clearly seen better times.

The market was a labyrinth of narrow alleys built around a lake of fetid vapor. Trolls of varying sizes, shapes, and ages squirmed past one another, ignoring the filth and meager offerings. Instead, trolls scavenged the crumbling marble shoreline, picking through garbage left by vendors who could care less, scattering vermin in their wake. Muddy water trickled down from above, from the streets of Brooklyn and the East River, forming cloudy puddles that people stepped in, not caring about the mud adding a new layer of grime to their boots, pants, and skin.

A huge machine with two monstrous steel rollers ground meat and bones which were distributed in grimy buckets to the avid customers. It appeared to be some manner of rationing, another indication of how far the fairy nation had fallen.

Hellboy was genuinely moved by the squalid conditions. He was also thrilled and amazed to be there. As the emotions battled within his heart and mind, he activated his communicator and spoke.

"Liz, you should be here."

His voice caught Krauss' attention, which tore his gaze from a vendor specializing in limbs, and he hissed, "Keep communications to a minimum—you'll blow our cover."

Hellboy looked about him, noting that they'd been exposed for over a minute. The troll that accompanied them had vanished into the crowds, as had the kitten, and no alarm had been sounded. He was not at all sure what the need for secrecy was all about so he happily ignored his superior and continued to chat.

"You would love it, Liz. No one's looking at us—we blend right in."

Liz smiled at her boyfriend's jubilant tone, picturing herself freely walking anywhere beside him and no one would care.

Before the image could form in her head, the channel crackled and Krauss said, "*Over and out.*" The circuit was closed.

She frowned at that. Sure, Abe, Hellboy, and Krauss got to mingle somewhere fantastic and she was left minding the store, sitting inside a fancy garbage truck and making small talk with Manning. She didn't dislike him, not the way Red did, but he wouldn't be the first person she'd think of to kill time with.

"I like the way he takes charge," Manning said, quite happy.

"You think?"

Manning smiled at that, missing her sarcasm. "He's efficient, and precise."

She tried again. "You add resistant to that and you got a new watch."

"Dr. Krauss is very aware of the chain of command and he seems to like me," the bureaucrat added. He sat back, fingering his ever-present roll of Tums but not eating any. He was too pleased with the way things were going. If only she would share that sensation.

"Manning?"

He glanced over, eager to continue their chat. "Yes?"

"Kissing ass leaves no minty aftertaste."

At that, she rose, working out a kink in her back, and hit the button that opened their exit. She stepped out into the cooling night air, glad to be away from Manning, but not at all happy to be alone in Brooklyn.

Liz decided to take a walk as she considered her sorry state of affairs. Before too long, she glanced up at a well-lit billboard that carried the catch phrase "A Big Decision."

Absently, her hand rubbed her abdomen.

It was a dizzying cacophony of sights and sounds, not to mention the smells, most of which were very unpleasant. Hellboy was perfectly happy to breathe through his mouth and avoid most of the odors. He also knew there'd be a long, hot bath when he got back to Jersey.

He marveled at the kiosks and shops, as they sold a meager supply of goods but an array the likes of which he'd never seen before. Hanging from a curved, wooden display were two rows of cats, both skinned and dried, as well as living ones.

No stall was especially large and all had clearly seen better days. They reeked and showed their age with bowed wooden shelves or frayed garments. Most vendors and shoppers seemed hunched over, shuffling from place to place, listlessly going through the motions. No one looked happy, he noted. Most had a hangdog look about them, partly from the way life had beaten them down and partly from their natural physiology.

Most kept covered up in thick robes, hiding their bodies. Many wore wooden masks obscuring their features and displaying fierce or happy visages painted onto the worn wood.

The goblins and trolls were of varying sizes, with most wandering vendors coming to his hip, and others dwarfing even Hellboy's size. One gargantuan creature was covered in a colorless blanket, lanterns hanging in two rows across its broad, slumped shoulders. In a woven basket, it carried its wares, an assortment of spices and cooking implements from the look of it.

Hellboy had never seen trolls and goblins hobnob with one another before and always assumed they didn't get along. Maybe here was a DMZ of sorts.

A vendor walked by him selling tadpoles on a stick which he presumed made for good snacks. He'd stick to Cheetos, though.

Following the tadpole troll was a mummy vendor with pieces of mummies, or rolls of the gauzy wrap they used, affixed to a tall board hoisted high in the air and balanced against a bony shoulder. Finally, a skin vendor followed him, offering different shades and textures, claiming they were well cleansed and disease free.

As they walked, the small group was ignored, just more oddities in a sea of oddities. If anything, the human Liz would stand out and be the object of stares. Maybe it was best she remained on the surface—at least this visit.

The entire market stretched as far as they could see and rose at least two or three stories into the air, until the curved rocky ceiling stopped it. Braziers, torches, and lanterns lit the streets, throwing pools of light every few feet. It was a dim light, but one that added to the downbeat atmosphere. Trolls slumped in doorways, sleeping off a binge or too weak to move. Others begged, sitting on tattered mats, empty bowls before them. One in particular had an infant cradled in its lap.

Not far ahead was a perennial market sight: an organ grinder complete with pet monster. The organ seemed made from the remains of some creature and the handle was clearly a bone. The sounds were shrill and barely musical but people tossed coins at his feet so it must work for the locals. The monster was demonic looking, a troll version of a monkey, with brightly colored hair and a short vest in blood reds and sickly blues. Like its counterpart, it wore a cute little hat.

Hellboy was taking in the sights, letting Krauss do the actual investigating. No doubt they'd find some clue as to where the tooth fairies came from, not that he saw any for sale. No doubt, they were bartered from backrooms within the buildings they passed.

As a result of his own absent-minded wandering, he did not notice his friend, Abe, who seemed fixated on a rag-encased figure. Had he paid any attention, he would have noticed she stood out like Liz would have given her shapely and diminutive form. She blended in, covered in the innocuous rags, but something about her movements captivated Abe's attention.

Had Hellboy looked further, he also would have noticed that when she turned, it was obvious how gorgeous she was for a human, amphibian, or troll. A more observant person, such as Abe, would also see that she wore a bracelet that was adorned with the royal seal's coat of arms.

As it was, Hellboy barely noticed that Abe set off in pursuit. The amphibian followed her into a building that sold primary-colored tinctures.

"Brother Red!"

Hellboy finally noticed Abe was out of sight and switched on his microphone. "Not now, Abe. I'm watching the über-investigator at work."

He and Krauss paused outside a spice shop, a small crumbling building that had rack after rack of spices in every color imaginable and some Hellboy would be hard pressed to name. The lead agent walked up to a troll and addressed him.

"Excuse me, sir, may I . . ."

His words were interrupted as the troll loudly roared and bumped Krauss aside, clearly not interested in talking to a gas bag. As Krauss tried to right himself, the next passerby, another fragglewump, pointedly bumped into him, knocking the Austrian further off balance.

When Krauss finally stood straight, it was clear the approach was wrong. Hellboy smothered a laugh and kept his face looking serious. With a gesture, Krauss squared his shoulders once more and entered the spice shop.

The shirtless owner was ugly but the smaller, second head he sported was even uglier. This troll was brawny and well-muscled on the left side but the right, where the second head resided, was withered and decayed looking, the right arm shrunken and more in proportion to the smaller head and shoulder that resided there. He manned the shop and he seemed to be making a blend from sixteen different spices; burlap bags and tiny glass bottles were scattered before him. The gnarled hands were working with ease; clearly, he'd done this particular mix before so he could afford to address his potential customers. A sneer formed on the troll's dry, cracked lips.

Carefully, Krauss reached into a pocket and withdrew a photograph of the dead tooth fairy and displayed it to the owner. "Excuse me, uh, sir, where can we purchase some of these?"

The two-headed troll stopped mixing his spices and studied the image briefly. "No one sells 'em down here, pal."

The lone customer in the shop with them was a huge round creature, with horns that curled down from its brow, ending with curled, sharp points. He had an upturned nose with slits for nostrils which opened into an oval mouth packed with spiked teeth. He seemed to be wearing some sort of leather and studded armor and his bulk was placed atop disproportionately tiny, but well muscled, legs. He waddled over, took one glance, and offered, "Over in Jersey, maybe."

That made both heads on the shopkeeper laugh and the giant creature joined in, the horrid sound filling the tiny confines.

Undaunted, Krauss took out a second picture, this of the royal seal that was found on the tooth fairy container.

"And what about this?" he asked. "Do you recognize this seal?"

Both looked at the picture and the owner clearly paled at the sight. "No, we don't," the troll replied.

Just outside the shop, the organ grinder played on. Neither B.P.R.D. agent noticed that the monkey-monster stopped dancing for coins but looked through the window and stared at the picture of the seal. It then dropped out of sight and moved through the crowd.

"Please, sir," Krauss pleaded in a tone Hellboy had not yet heard. Could it be the famed agent from Washington was going to strike out and didn't want to look bad on his first case?

The owner leaned down, returning to his special blends of herbs and spices. Without looking at Krauss, he said, "You'd better go. *Now.*"

Firmly, Krauss said, "We'll make it worth your while."

The hulking figure leaned over Krauss, his breath fogging part of the glass dome that served as the agent's head. "Don't waste your time. We will not talk."

That got Hellboy's attention. It was one thing for Krauss to fail for being a pain in the neck. It was something else for him to be threatened. He stepped closer to the crony and addressed him.

"You're absolutely sure of that?"

"Absolutely," the creature said, puffing out his already massive chest.

"Oh, yeah?"

"Yeah." He raised his arms, scraping the low ceiling and towering over both Krauss and Hellboy. Were Manning here, he'd be wetting his pants or running away—but not Hellboy.

"All right, then."

Without much of a windup, Hellboy reared back and his oversized right fist came flying around and made contact with the offered jaw. The creature was big, but soft, and the force of the blow literally knocked him out of his boots. Flying backward and landing roughly on his back, the creature destroyed a wall of shelved spices, which shattered and spilled all over him, coating him in a riot of color.

As the interrogation proceeded, Hellboy would later learn, Abe had trailed the figure into the Map Bazaar, a maze of alleys ending in a small square. The antiquarian shops dealt with the mysteries of the troll world, from parchment fragments to maps that led to places only whispered about in the taverns.

He had followed the woman and watched from a discreet distance as she sought a specific shop. Once she found her goal, an ochre building with maps and scrolls filling a window, she entered it without looking back.

To avoid detection, Abe lingered on the square's periphery and concentrated on the melody coming from a different organ grinder who had a pet monster, instead of a monkey. Still, Abe later told his friend that the music was actually good and worthy of a tip. He had brought with him some change and

tipped the performer, earning him a good-natured smile from
the monster, who actually tipped his Turkish-style hat in Abe's
direction.

Satisfied sufficient time had passed, Abe drew closer to the
building and watched the woman, in profile, agitatedly negoti-
ate with a recalcitrant shopkeeper. The back and forth seemed
to exasperate both of them until she finally raised a hand to
call the arguing to a halt.

The other hand rose and removed the bracelet from her arm
and handed it to the shopkeeper for study. He brought it close
to his slitted eyes and his entire manner changed. Abe watched
in fascination as it became clear the symbols meant something
to him and he bowed low and calmed down in an instant.
Now he raised a hand, asking her for patience. He then walked
out of sight.

A moment later, he returned, showing off a fat crystal
cylinder that filled his hand. The other hand held a leather
carrying case, sized to match the cylinder, and Abe grew
curious.

Hellboy, though, was not done with his own investigation.
At the spice shop, he shifted his shoulders, settling his overcoat
into place, and turned his attention to the two-headed troll.
Both mouths had dropped open and both faces looked discolored. Hellboy leaned across the table, blew mightily, scattering
the blend in progress, and then backhanded the troll so both
heads banged into the back wall.

Krauss seemed to know better and remained quiet and in
place, letting Hellboy take the lead for a change. Encouraged,
Hellboy opened his hand flat and smacked the larger of the
two heads back and forth. After several blows, teeth had been
loosened and several flew from the man's mouth.

"Feeling more chatty now?" Hellboy asked him.

"Yessss! Yesss! Don't—don't hit me—all right?"

The smaller head finally spoke up, its voice pitched differently and sounding smaller. "It's rumors!"

That earned him a quizzical look from Hellboy who merely gestured for either head to continue.

"They say that Prince Nuada broke the truce . . . sent a message to world above," the larger head said, spitting out blood and mucous.

That brought Krauss closer to the exchange and he leaned forward, urgently asking, "A message?"

"Of war," the smaller head replied, sounding absolutely terrified of what was to come.

"He left his emblem in the world above and now there's talk of war," the larger head added. "A war against the human world."

Krauss stood still, absorbing and processing the new information. Hellboy recognized this was bad. Any war was bad but war with fairies, trolls, goblins, and other creatures sounded particularly bad. He finally flashed on the memories he had been struggling to recall. His mind was filled with snow, a Christmas tree, and a particularly worrisome story Broom had told him in New Mexico.

It was time to assemble the troops. He looked beyond the spice shop and couldn't find his friend.

Hellboy asked Krauss, "Where's Abe?"

Krauss stared at him silently.

As they exchanged looks, Hellboy's hand slipped to his belt and activated the locator, hoping the fish-man was safe.

CHAPTER TWELVE

Everything about the Troll Market fascinated Abe. It was a treasure trove of artifacts to confirm or correct information he possessed in the library of books he had more or less inherited from Professor Broom.

He felt Broom's absence rather keenly. Certainly not as much as Red did, but he and Broom had had decades of stimulating conversations and debates, countless games of chess, and had shared many adventures. Broom was one of the first humans to accept him unconditionally, which was a vast improvement from the first decades of his life.

The void Broom's death created was hard for Abe, since neither Hellboy or Liz really shared his fascination with the paranormal history that so interested him. Sure, they shared many mutual interests and the three had grown quite close, especially after Liz moved back to B.P.R.D. headquarters. Still, he missed the intellectual debate.

Krauss appeared to be a stimulating companion and could be the one to fill the void. He appreciated Krauss's intellect and devotion to order. Yes, maybe the Austrian gentleman adhered too closely to the rules but being based in Washington and not being in the field would do that to anyone. Red just needed to give the man time to adjust.

Another void gaped in his heart, Abe realized. It was one he rarely let himself think about but once he saw this woman, it was all he could think about. There were no other amphibians he knew of, no one with whom he could fully share his life. The notions of love were certainly beyond his reach and experience; yet, the moment he spotted her, something clicked. His heart skipped a beat and he found he could not take his eyes off of her.

There was a word for it, something he had learned from Hellboy.

Twitterpated.

That was it. He didn't know her name but he was most definitely twitterpated.

When his belt buckle started to glow blue, he was genuinely annoyed at being interrupted. He glanced at the buckle, knowing that the others sought him, but he wasn't ready to depart. He thumbed it off and looked back at the window.

She had vanished.

"Oh," he said aloud and with great disappointment.

He decided to go shopping and headed for the store. As he crossed the distance, he did not hear the low growl coming from a shadowy corner. Abe had totally missed that his observance of the mysterious woman was being watched by Wink.

The door faintly chimed as he entered and the odor of ancient texts was as welcome to him as coming home. He paused to admire the disorderly piles of scrolls, maps, books, and hung parchments. The proprietor, a hunchbacked figure of indeterminate age and species, but clearly comfortable in his surroundings, looked his way and nodded in greeting.

Abe could see himself lingering here for hours, spending every coin in his pockets to purchase these rare treasures for preservation back in the library. One unrolled scroll was spread across a chest-high table, each end held by golden busts of minotaurs. He turned to see what had been drawn but a voice caught him by surprise. It was feminine and lovely, but also was backed with steel.

"Why are you following me?"

It was *her*. His heart beat faster and if he were human, he would probably have started to sweat.

She had removed the rag-covered cloak and was standing resplendent in gleaming azure robes made from fine silks. There was not a trace of dirt or grime on her compared with the other denizens of the market so she stood out even further. The woman practically shone in the room and she was lovely. Her pale, alabaster-like skin was smooth and ageless. Her reddish eyes were captivating. The pointed tips to her ears were exotic. He had to say something.

"I—I was not . . ." Not smooth, not at all.

She glared at the stammering and quickly withdrew a dagger that was hidden in a fold by her dainty waist. It was sharp, he could tell, and the way she handled the weapon proved she was an adept. His heart continued to thud against his chest and Abe found he needed to control his breathing. After all, his collar contained only so much water.

"Did my brother send you?" she demanded, stepping even closer. *My god, was she wearing perfume*, Abe thought. *What did she just ask?*

"Your brother? You are sorely mistaken."

That didn't seem to satisfy her so she moved even closer and this time, the tip of the dagger rested against his chin, confirming how sharp a blade it was.

She met his eyes steadily and asked once more. "Then answer me truthfully. Why were you following me?"

"My name is Abe Sapien." He couldn't think clearly so he was going to deal only with the truth and with luck it would set him free.

"There is no such name!" she snapped.

"Oh, I don't like it either, but . . ."

She interrupted him and said, "Enough. Give me your hand."

Abe blinked, uncertain why she would want to hold hands.

"Your hand," she repeated, her tone indicating he really didn't have a choice.

Slowly, he raised his right hand and she gripped it, turning it over and lightly running her fingertips over the palm. It tingled and he luxuriated in the gentleness of her fingers. She possessed power, one not dissimilar to his telepathic prowess and he opened up his mind to let her explore. In so doing, she unknowingly offered him a glimpse in reverse and he reveled in it. Other than the dagger still at his throat, this was rather pleasant.

She gasped once and then said in an astonished tone, "You're an agent of the Bureau for Paranormal Research and Defense. And your name is—is—oh . . ."

He nodded in agreement. "Horrible. I know."

Satisfied, she lowered the dagger and in a blink it was once more out of sight. She also released his hand, which caused him a pang of regret. The woman withdrew a pace and then addressed him with some formality.

"I am Nuala. Princess Nuala."

It was not a name he knew from the annals but it was something he recognized from moments before when their minds had brushed against one another. He nodded in confirmation and said, "I know. Forgive me, Your Highness. But, as you learned about me, I couldn't help but learn a little bit about you myself."

She stared at him with new eyes, interested.

"I know that you need our help."

There, it was said and out in the open. She sighed once and agreed. In fact, Nuala now seemed to totally relax around him, the "royalness" seeping away and the woman coming through. Walking about the tiny map shop, she gestured helplessly.

"I'm afraid it's the other way around."

That caught his attention. She clearly had gleaned more from him than he from her and he was bewildered. Nuala seemed ready to explain when a sound caught their attention. Both turned toward the door and it splintered apart as Wink burst through, wider than the doorway.

He already had his metallic hand disengaged and began to spin it in the tiny confines, creating gusts that scattered loose papers every which way. Nuala shrank back and Abe suddenly wished he had Red's Samaritan.

The hand slashed through the air and ripped into the walls, tearing delicate parchment decorations, ripping wallpaper into confetti and creating deep gouges in the wood. Wink whirled it again and lashed forward as Abe ducked and a cabinet full of scrolls toppled over, cracking as it impacted the floor. By then, the shopkeeper had run out a back door and Abe wanted to follow but was cut off by the hulking form.

Hanging oil lamps were knocked to the ground and in a moment something was going to catch fire from a burning lamp and should the shop go up, the loss would be incalculable.

Rather than worry about the loss of the maps, he turned his attention to Nuala, who scampered to the far wall and reached up to grab the edges of a window. Smoothly, she clambered up and through while Wink directed his rage at Abe. The artificial hand whipped around once more and the amphibian tried to avoid it, but the creature seemed to have anticipated that and adjusted as he let the hand fly like a mace.

It struck Abe directly in the face, threatening to crack his goggles, and the impact knocked him back, ass over teakettle, so to speak. In fact, he staggered back and wound up falling through a different window.

Abe had to thank Wink for the blow, because it brought him back to his senses and by sending him out of the building, freed him to fight on his own terms. He regained his feet and controlled his excited breathing as Wink emerged from the now-burning shop.

The creature stalked Abe who calmly stood at the ready. He thought briefly about where Nuala might have gone and how he would find her to learn what she had intimated. Then, arms and legs spread, he was ready to handle Wink.

Having grown up in the water and learned to walk, run, and swim both under and above the water, he had perfected his own style of fighting. It was part martial arts, part ballet, and all his. Abe called it the "Way of the Water" and it had proven most effective through the years. For every punch Wink sent his way, Abe easily avoided it and as he moved away, landed his own strikes. Given his opponent's biped form, Abe anticipated where nerve clusters and pressure points might be and exploited those.

Wink would swing and Abe would reach up into the armpit and numb the arm. Each failed blow caused Wink to bellow, filling the air with a terrible sound. In some ways, it was more effective than the belt locator.

Wink did have one advantage over Abe and that was stamina. He needed to end this quickly, so the next time Wink struck out, Abe managed to land a kick to the creature's larynx, knocking him backward. Wink crashed into a fairy coop, cracking it open and spilling out malnourished fairies that flew freely away.

The organ grinder's monster was watching in fascination although Abe had no sight of the grinder himself. Instead, he needed to duck as the whirling metallic hand came hurtling in his direction. Once more he deftly rolled out of the way as the hand connected with a limestone column.

At that moment, Abe grabbed nearby trunks and threw them, one at a time, toward his attacker. Each trunk contained powdered dyes and suddenly the raging beast was covered in cyan, magenta, and yellow dust.

He bellowed then growled something in a language Abe had not heard before. Wink was calling to someone or something, and was pointing to a specific alley, but he had no clue who or what, so he decided it was time to bring things to an end.

Abe missed the nod of recognition Wink received from the organ grinder's pet monster, who scurried into the designated alley's shadows to obey the order.

While Wink concentrated on regaining his hand, Abe moved away, seeking an alley escape of his own. He glanced up and spotted a shining arm waving toward him. It was Nuala, who had not run away but sought shelter and awaited him. This gladdened his heart although, to his mind, it complicated his own actions.

He dashed into the alley and together, the pair ran to the opposite end and found an archway to hide under. Her gleaming robes were hard to hide but he put as much of himself between her and exposure as possible. They were close, and he felt her warmth, took comfort and strength from it.

Wink drew closer to their position and trolls, goblins, and other shoppers scattered in any direction that took them far from the angry stalker. His hand adjusted the artificial weapon on his wrist and Wink seemed ready to pummel Abe and the princess into paste. They had nowhere to run and their hiding spot inhibited Abe's ability to fight.

The metal hand was drawn back, about to deliver the killing blow, and a deadly grin crossed Wink's face.

Two rapid shots resounded through the air, both hitting the hand, resounding loudly in the silence. Sparks glowed brightly upon contact.

Abe dared to look past a stunned and injured Wink. Sure enough, standing as proudly as ever, was Hellboy, actually taking the time to light a victory cigar. Krauss was behind him, but clearly, the lead agent was letting Red do the heavy lifting.

Smart man.

"Let me put this as delicately as I can," Hellboy said to Wink.

He then stepped closer, lowering the Samaritan and taking aim. Wink stood defiant, refusing to back down. Behind him were bins filled with liquid and fabric being dyed. They were all punctured, leaking colorful water onto the street, creating a rainbow stream that flowed near Wink's feet.

Hellboy pulled the trigger and that forced Wink to step further back, closer to the vats. The creature was quick, though, and raised his arm to let the metal hand deflect the killing shots.

With a wicked grin, Wink stepped forward, swinging the dented but functional hand right into Hellboy's face. The impact made Abe sympathetically wince.

"Mmh." An unintelligible sound from Hellboy.

That was an invitation for the two to brawl, more evenly matched than Abe ever could be and he was just fine with that. Nuala stepped from behind him and marveled at their savior, no doubt knowing who he was from her telepathic tour of his mind.

Given the confines of the market, the two brawlers fairly destroyed kiosks, stalls, and even building storefronts as arms swung, curses flew and bodies were sent flying. Wink's metal hand went through the air, Hellboy ducked, and an entire display of freshly hacked demon limbs was obliterated; the troll holding it over his head crumbled to the ground, fearing for his life.

Hellboy took several brutal body blows, usually laughing or politely grunting, which encouraged Abe that his friend was not overmatched. Red zipped right past him and settled atop a pile of freshly dyed blue fabric. Seeing his coat and pants now splotched in blue, Hellboy roared in anger and threw himself at Wink, the force carrying them both right through one stall and into a store that might have sold ceramic containers—tomorrow it would only peddle shards.

"Now you pissed me off," Hellboy announced, lighting a fresh cigar.

He flicked the match away and as Wink momentarily looked at the smoking stick, Hellboy took advantage of the distraction to hurl himself into Wink's midsection, sending them tumbling to the ground, a tangle of arms and legs. They rolled near the ruined dyeing area and splashed amidst the pools of colorful liquid, each looking like funhouse-mirror versions of themselves.

Wink got to his feet first and grabbed his opponent by the shoulders, roughly tossing Hellboy against two marble pillars. Working quickly, he then projected his steel fist and yanked Hellboy off the ground and sent him through a hanging arch-way. Red fell heavily and Abe imagined how sore he was going to be when this was over.

Hellboy got back on his feet and winced only once before charging Wink again. Fighting in close quarters once more, it was fist against fist as steel battled stone. Hellboy's natural stone right hand proved mightier as it pounded away, actually denting the artificial hand and bending the metal inward.

Wink roared in frustration and anger, staring in wonderment at his ruined hand. Once again, Hellboy took advantage and gathered himself, clasping his hands together, and delivered a powerful uppercut that not only knocked Wink onto his back, but seemed to actually take the fight out of him.

"I think we're done . . . give it up," Hellboy admonished the creature.

Wink, from the ground, growled and released his fist chain at Hellboy.

"You know? I wouldn't do that if I were you," he told Wink.

Wink roared and resumed standing, swirling his dented mace around and around his head. Finally, he released it at Hellboy. Wink's steel fist sailed past the sidestepping Red and landed right at the edge of the nearby meat-grinding machine. It was still operating despite the carnage around it and a dented bit of fist got caught up in the roller, carrying the entire fist and then chain into the mechanism. The meat-grinding-machine rollers were designed for demon meats, tougher to process than mere farm animals, and that meant the machine was incredibly powerful. Wink never stood a chance, despite yanking and pulling, his feet skidding against the dirt and slipping in a puddle. Inexorably, he came closer to the machine. Even as he continued to struggle, his strength finally beginning to flag, Wink reached the machine and got a close look at the grinding metal teeth that were chewing up his chain like spaghetti.

"Toldya," Hellboy said as Wink moved past him and reached the machine.

The rollers chewed onward and Wink was finally drawn in. His screaming was no doubt heard all over the market and Abe covered his sensitive ears. Soon, there was nothing of the creature left exposed and the machinery continued to chew Wink up, processing him into consumable meat that some might find a bit stringy. Below the machine, Abe noted red, blue, and yellow dye seeping out, mixing with the offal from previous creatures processed earlier that day. Finally, at the other end of the mammoth construction, a flattened piece of armor, recognizably Wink's, spewed forth.

Once the screaming had died out, people began to peer from behind destroyed stalls or through shattered windows. Satisfied the fight was over, trolls and goblins emerged and began the process of restoring order and getting back to the business of buying and selling. It wasn't long before the music of one, then two, organ grinders could be heard.

Krauss approached Hellboy and the two stood wordlessly beside one another. Abe decided with the danger over, he should get the team back on the case. He had a sense time was not on their side. He gestured for Nuala to follow him and the two joined the agents. Krauss nodded toward Abe and Hellboy just gaped at the pretty princess. Nuala stood, used to being introduced by others.

"Red—Dr. Krauss, this is Princess Nuala."

Hellboy glanced at Abe and shot him a questioning look. He ignored his friend and continued.

"The princess needs our help."

Hellboy was about to ask a question when he was cut off.

"I'm afraid it's the other way around."

As the fight had progressed, the pet monster had scampered off, following Wink's final instructions. It found its way to Nuada's chambers, tucked out of sight and difficult to access in an obscure corner of the market. The space was a tight fight, but comfortably appointed as befitted a rogue prince. He was working at a table, a lantern flickering light near his busy hands. Bits and pieces of metal, gears, and springs were scattered about as he worked toward the completion of a unique delivery device. Hearing the monster's approach, he paused, a shriveled bean in the palm of his hand.

The creature doffed its hat in obeisance and received a welcoming nod from the prince.

"Is there something you need to tell me?" he asked the pet.

While the pet explained Wink's situation, his twin sister stood awkwardly under the combined stare of Krauss and Hellboy. When she began her story, Krauss led them out of the market, wisely presuming that Wink's master might be nearby. They would be better protected back up on the surface, with Liz and Manning, inside a well-defended lab truck. The withdrawal from the market made Abe a little sad; there was so much he still wanted to see and sample. He had yet to buy a single artifact for himself. Abe vowed he would return some day soon.

The exit went without incident and Nuala continued to tell her tale, in great detail and with a formal language that impressed Abe. She had been trained to be at court, and this now enabled her to properly explain the state of affairs in the fairy kingdom. They paused to briefly try and restore the huge steel door that sealed the market from the world. It had been ruined and would need to be replaced, something Abe doubted they could handle from petty cash. He felt they owed it to the trolls to leave them be, even though her words of impending war were chilling him.

The walk back up the tunnel was hard and he was tiring. No doubt, she too was fatigued and Hellboy let out the occasional grunt indicating he was aching. Still, nothing challenged them and they easily accessed the refrigerated meat locker. Nuala paused to finish her story, wishing to show them some actual proof of her account. They were at ease with her, which pleased Abe. He even entertained notions they'd help her, or she'd help them, and then maybe, just maybe, she'd come to stay at the B.P.R.D. headquarters. She'd love the books in Broom's library, of that he was certain.

What she had told them sounded more like the plot to some cheesy cable movie, not a true threat to the world beyond the market.

To punctuate her story, though, Nuala withdrew the final piece of the crescent crown and displayed it. Krauss seemed convinced, which pleased Abe. They both understood the legends and the history of the pact, matching it against other legends they had both learned through the years. If the ages-old truce was truly torn asunder, mankind had no way of knowing it was about to go to war. Unlike terrorists or fascists, these were people fighting for their very existence. The fight would use machines too terrifying to describe and the notion of goblins overrunning the nation's capitol was an image Abe wanted to blot from his mind.

"To wage war, my brother needs this," she said of the golden arc in her hand. "The last of the three pieces of the crown of Bethmoora."

Returning the piece to her belt, Nuala then withdrew the crystal cylinder she had recently obtained and displayed it to their curious eyes. Abe picked it up from her hand and carefully examined it, amazed at its construction and detail. He couldn't begin to imagine its age or how it was made, but knew it was one of a kind and therefore needed to be protected. Wink was no doubt not the only ally Nuada had at his disposal.

"And the secret location of the Golden Army chamber—meant to be found within this cylinder."

Krauss nodded in comprehension as he thought for a moment and then added, "The Golden Army. The harbingers of death—the unstoppable tide . . ."

The army meant something to Hellboy, Abe realized. The look of familiarity was obvious, but Red, staring off into the distance, muttered, "Howdy Doody." Whatever that was, it meant something only to his friend. He could ask about it later—now it was time to act.

Krauss seemed to be on the same wavelength because he turned to the princess and gestured at the cylinder.

"Your highness, if you hand the crown piece over to us . . ."

She cut him off, shaking her head firmly in the negative. "Where it goes, I go . . . my father died to uphold the truce with your world." He was not at all surprised and inexplicably proud of her.

Hellboy snapped out of his daze and once more re-engaged with the others. Something about the truce caught his attention and Abe was happy to have his friend's support. If they were to take on the world of fairies, they needed to be in this together. He could only imagine what Manning would think about an impending war.

"You must honor his noble intention," she said to Krauss. Hellboy, though, nodded in agreement.

"The lady is in dire danger," Abe said, feeling instantly foolish for stating the obvious.

Krauss turned his attention to Abe and asked directly, "You're vouching for her, I take it, Agent Sapien?"

"Oh, most emphatically, yes."

Shaking his domed head slowly, Krauss replied, "Even so, I'm sorry. We cannot assume such responsibility on our own."

Abe was stunned. He was about to protest, but Hellboy moved faster, pressing his face up against the glass bubble where the swirling gases seemed agitated.

"She lost her father—what else do you need?" Hellboy demanded.

"There are procedures—rules—you can't just . . ." Krauss was actually stammering, stuck on the rule book. Fortunately, Hellboy used the rule book more as a doorstop than a guide.

With dramatic emphasis, Hellboy said, "She's coming with us, Fishbowl."

"Damn straight," Abe agreed.

A sound caught his attention and he looked up, noting a shadow approach the entrance to the locker. The shadow was attached to a male version of Nuala, complete with finery and the royal seal. This had to be the mad prince, Nuada. The one who threatened man's world with Armageddon.

"Sister, I see you keep good company." His voice was firm and strong, rich in timbre and actually pleasing to hear. The emotion, though, was cold, and Abe knew him to be a genuine threat.

"Who did this to my loyal friend?"

He tossed the flattened armor, still dyed in blue, yellow, red, and blood, at their feet. It clanged loudly in the mostly metal locker area.

Hellboy stepped forward and gestured at himself. "I'm right here, pal. Talk to me."

Nuada appraised Hellboy with a single glance and then proclaimed, "Born out of a womb of shadows. Thrown into their world and you still think you belong."

Hellboy disliked hearing others discuss his origins or the realm of birth. Abe worried that Hellboy would once more act impulsively and he doubted the prince would fall as easily as his minion, Wink, did.

"Are we gonna talk all night? Cause I'm sleepy," he said by way of challenge.

"You will pay for what you've done," Nuada promised but did not make a move. Nuala stepped behind Abe, concerned about what was to happen next.

She had every reason to be concerned as the Samaritan was brought into view, casually pointed at the prince. Hellboy said to him, "Do you take checks?"

Abe expected Nuada to react to the threat, probably with a sword. No doubt, the prince was well taught and experienced. Sword versus bullets usually favored the gunslinger but not necessarily this time.

The prince, though, reached into his robes and withdrew an oval, mechanical device. He felt the princess stiffen behind him, which meant she recognized it and this was nothing good.

"No, brother—no!" she cried.

Too late. The prince had activated the grenade and they could all hear it softly tick until the countdown was complete. The golden device whirred and clicked, then split apart, well-oiled springs letting it open without a sound. Within was a large peach-pit-sized item that seemed more seed than explosive. It was green and huge and not at all threatening, but if the princess was worried, then Abe shared her concern. He just wished he knew why.

Hellboy snorted and said, "Somebody stop that man—he has a *bean!*"

The prince, not taking his eyes off Red, brought the seed up to his lips and in a soft voice commanded, "*Kill him.*"

At that, the grenade released the bean and it rolled to the floor and proceeded to roll away from the refrigerated space, toward the street.

Nuala moved around Abe, her arms outstretched, and she screamed, "Get it! Get it!!"

Abe was at her side, moving after the bean. As he neared it, he bent low to grab it with his webbed right hand but as he approached, the bean darted away. Could it be sentient, he wondered.

Hellboy followed Abe, leaving Krauss near the prince. Krauss wondered how wise that was. Still, he could tell Red wasn't taking the threat at all seriously. Clearly, the bean was dangerous, given the delivery device and the very fact the prince wielded it in revenge for Wink's death. He wished Hellboy would occasionally stop and consider these facts, but now was most certainly not the time to get into this with him. If the princess wanted the bean retrieved, then she knew what it was and that was good enough for him.

"Relax—it's a *jumping bean*," Hellboy said as he caught up to them.

"Hurry!" Nuala called.

As they charged after the rapidly moving bean, which seemed to be gaining a lead, Hellboy glanced behind him to see if the prince was gloating, but he was nowhere to be seen. All he saw was Krauss running to catch up.

The bean left the locker and was out in the abandoned meat-packing facility and seemed to be homing in on a wet metal drain, built into the floor, covered with grit and cobwebs. The bean barely paused at the lip of the drain and then hopped into the air, surprising Abe.

"It's going for the water!"

Bean. Water. Abe did not like where this was leading. He reached one final time to grab it in midair but the seed rose higher than he expected and then arced down through a slot in the drain and moments later, they all heard the plop of bean meeting water.

"Oh, my god, we must go back up—evacuate the area!" Nuala was nearing hysteria and that worried Abe something fierce.

"Gimme a break, willya? It's just a . . ." Abe was worried, because Hellboy's annoyed comments were cut off by a very deep, very ominous rumble coming from the drain. Within instants, the flooring trembled, vibrating faster and faster, indicating something was coming up from below, and fast. The entire room was shaking and no doubt the building would follow.

Abe began to think the first shot in the war against humanity had just been fired.

CHAPTER THIRTEEN

The rumbling sound reached the street and alarmed Liz and Manning. They quickly checked their viewscreens and saw nothing obvious. Liz then accessed the lab's sensory equipment and still couldn't figure out what was happening. This part of Brooklyn was nowhere near a power plant or fault line. Yet, the energy required to shake bedrock, concrete, brick, and asphalt had to be considerable.

With the lab equipment showing nothing but the vibrations increasing, Liz decided it was time to get out of the truck. Manning followed, making inarticulate sounds that couldn't quite become words or questions but indicated a level of stress. She doubted the Tums would be effective right now.

The other B.P.R.D. agents were already fanned out on the streets, looking for some obvious evidence of the cause. All wore identical looks of caution, concern, and panic. They all looked toward Manning, the officer in charge with Krauss below, and he looked back with wide eyes, his downturned mouth glued shut, offering no direction, let alone leadership.

Things felt worse now and she was certain the vibration was coming from below them and rising, more like an earthquake than, say, a detonation. But what could be coming through the ground? Was it related to the hunt for the Troll

Market? She thought there was a likely connection but she couldn't imagine what it was.

Whatever late-night traffic there was had stopped. Cars didn't dare move closer to buildings that might collapse or even the bridge they feared would tumble down. People craned their necks or left their vehicles, uncertain of what to do or where to go. Join the club, she mused.

Nearby, several lampposts sparked with overloaded energy and the bulbs exploded with showers of sparks that lit the night air. That caused cries of concern and people were now leaning out of apartment windows, seeking answers.

They were rewarded with the sound of cracking pavement, stone, and tar bursting apart, rising up, pushed by what appeared to be a dark green tendril. No, it was a vine—Liz spotted leaves sprouting from the sides. Some giant plant was rising out of a Brooklyn street. She gaped at it, trying to calculate if she might possess enough firepower to take it out.

Her thoughts were interrupted as the vine, now free, rose faster and grew in girth. It ruptured more of the street, sending cars flying into the air. She watched in horror as one pirouetted through the air, crashing back to earth atop a steel hot-dog cart. Oil tanks that were holding fires to warm the homeless were sent rolling down the street, trailing flaming debris that ignited wrappers and other street refuse. People screamed, one trying to outdo the other, and others ran as far from the towering plant as was practical.

It kept growing and actually was threatening to smack into the underside of the bridge. Liz went cold at the notion. If that thing could smash through the ground, the bridge and its late-night users had no chance.

Sure enough, it kept right on growing and it first brushed the underside, then kept pushing, straining against it, gaining in girth at the same time. The thing was powerful, a living thing that seemed endless. Metal, wire, and electric cabling all snapped, all useless impediments to the plant. Once it pushed through the structure, it rose right past the road and she heard cars screeching. The distinctive sound of rubber tires trying to stop on a dime was matched by the metal on metal sound as cars no doubt smacked into one another. She dreaded the thought that if this had happened at rush hour, it would have crushed countless lives. Right now, though, there were still enough people being swatted aside inside their vehicles that the sounds of chaos continued. The thing continued to grow as she watched the top fronds poke into view. In fact, now that it cleared the bridge and rose above the span, it seemed to slow and blossom. The top fronds spread out, growing leaves and vines, becoming downright bushy.

She looked about, seeking the other agents, most of whom were aiding the injured. Good for them, she thought.

A glance toward the meat-packing facility showed Hellboy, Abe, Krauss, and some albino woman running toward her. They looked as concerned and bewildered as she felt and for a moment she allowed herself a moment's pleasure that clearly Red wasn't the cause of this. The quartet, though, did seem to know more than she did so she quickly crossed to them, pausing only to let a falling car hit the pavement right between her and Hellboy. She pitied the poor driver and hoped he or she had felt nothing. The car was a crumbled heap of steel and rubber, leaking fluids and rocking to a stop.

"What the hell was that?"

Hellboy was about to speak but stopped as he, Abe, and the others backed away. Three or four other cars came raining down and splattered all around them. The street was ruined, the bridge was wrecked and each passing second brought more death and destruction down around their heads.

Whatever caused this meant business. She only hoped they had a solution.

The vine, or rather stalk, continued to tower over them but seemed to have reached its growth limit but anything that strong was dangerous. Cutting it down was going to take an army.

Manning joined them and looked right at Hellboy and demanded, "Oh—what have you done now?"

The princess spoke up with an answer. "It's an *elemental*. A forest god."

Liz gaped at the attractive woman, uncertain of who she was or how she knew about the paranormal, but then again, this was just par for the course these days.

At the base of the plant, the vines revealed that they were actually coils of tightly wrapped leaves which were now loosening. They actually were splitting apart, revealing layers of fiber and bubbly looking stuff that seemed wrapped around a specific object. As the unfurling continued, it revealed a vaguely humanoid shape in the center.

They all turned to look at her then swiveled to look at the elemental. In the center of the shape a small green glow began to pulsate and then grew in intensity. Liz suddenly realized it was a heartbeat and that meant the thing was alive and would soon wake up. It was easily five stories tall and anything that big and strong spelled doom for the borough and anything else it wanted to wreck.

With every quickening heartbeat, more people decided to scream in panic and run away, filling the street with chaos. The B.P.R.D. agents were overwhelmed but did what they could while their colorful leadership gaped, powerless to stop the thing.

Hellboy announced in a matter-of-fact tone, "I'm gonna get me *Big Baby*."

Okay, Liz thought, that actually made sense. She watched him jog to the garbage truck and enter it, emerging moments later with the four-barreled pistol-gripped shotgun nicknamed Big Baby. It boasted six barrels clustered around a main axle, resembling nothing so much as a Gatling gun in miniature.

While he was inside, the first of several television news helicopters swooped overhead and trained its bright lights on the elemental, which was thankfully unaware of their presence. Or was it? As more arrived and additional lights were cast, the head reacted and looked in their direction.

Liz realized this was not good. Not good at all.

"Yeaaaaah! Come here," Hellboy called as he raised the rifle and took aim at the humongous thing.

It heard his voice amidst all the other sounds which spoke of superior hearing and maybe intelligence. The thing began to writhe, breaking free of the final strands of fiber that had housed it. One step was followed by a second and suddenly it was mobile. It proved to be swift and before Red could get off a single shot, the thing bent low and swiveled one huge arm down, its fist crushing the B.P.R.D.'s garbage truck/lab into so much scrap metal.

The thing then scooped up the crumbled metallic shape and hefted it into the air, having aimed at the nearest helicopter. It must still be orienting itself since the shot missed—not by much, but enough to spare the chopper and its crew. Wisely, the helicopter lifted higher and banked away from the action. The others were also in motion. Good, she thought, one less headache to deal with.

Abe managed to reach into his box of reference books, something that had emerged unscathed and Liz imagined it had been charmed somehow. He stood next to the pretty woman, whatever princess she claimed to be, and he read from it. Before he could share, a swinging elemental frond scattered them and they went running. Interestingly, Abe grabbed Nuala's hand as they ran. Everything about them indicated Abe was infatuated with her. That was most certainly odd, not something she'd ever seen before. It weirded her out, the notion that Abe was attracted to anyone.

The various vines that composed part of the elemental's body seemed to wriggle and move of their own volition, seeking people to destroy. Abe and Nuala huddled behind a building, both their backs pressed flat, and Abe held up a pistol. It was surely a useless gesture as no single bullet was going to slow down something that large, that alien.

The creature did act defensively as it continued to pick cars off the bridge and street as if they were cherries, ripe for eating. Or tossing. It picked up a dark blue Chevy and hurled it toward where Abe and Nuala were huddled. They knew to get out of its way and they ran further from the elemental. They narrowly missed being hit by the car as it crumpled into the street, digging a nice new pothole. Abe then grabbed the princess's hand and led her in a zigzag pattern as more cars came flying through the air. Liz noted the indiscriminate way the creature was working, tossing everything from a Lexus to a Kia at them, each one coming just a bit closer as it refined its aim.

After one particular near miss, from a Saturn no less, Abe let go so they could both run flat out and that proved to make the difference as a BMW came sailing in on their heels.

Then it got smart. The elemental tossed the next car over their heads and it landed in front of them, with the next one landing behind them. If they weren't quick, they'd be penned in and then surely crushed. Nuala, unused to cars Liz guessed, let Abe lead the way and direct their course of action. Of course, Abe might have been more comfortable had the thing been tossing yachts their way, but they'd have to deal.

They were a compact car away from being trapped when Abe yelled something at the princess, who nodded in agreement. Then, they threw themselves through the narrow gap remaining between death and freedom. The final car, a minivan for emphasis, came flying through the air as they dove forward. A tire and pieces of molding came flying free and smacked Abe on the legs as he tumbled just out of reach.

Abe stood and helped the princess get to her feet, ever the gentleman of course, and they met up with a panicked Manning.

She wanted to cheer, but couldn't pause to enjoy their salvation since the elemental was still on the move, still a danger to everyone. At least Krauss, Manning, Abe, and Nuala were all together. Liz went to join them, feeling safety in numbers was what was required.

Sure enough, the elemental continued to wend its way through Brooklyn, ripping apart brick buildings that had been built over a century before. Stray electric wires fell over it with little effect. In fact, no substance seemed to have any effect on it. It was moving in a line, causing massive destruction and death but it was also seeking something.

Or someone.

The elemental began to turn and then ponderously stalked Hellboy.

Raising Big Baby in his huge hand, Hellboy took aim and fired off four rapid shots. Each large-caliber round found its way into the thing's chest and the elemental kept moving forward, without pause, unharmed.

"So much for that," he said to himself.

As they scurried down the street, a woman approached them, her coat torn in two and hanging limply from her body. She was bleeding from various scratches but it was the hysteria in her eyes that made them pause.

"My baby! Help! The door's stuck! My baby is in there!"

She gestured feebly behind her, at a van crushed in various places, glass blown out and tires punctured. There was no way a normal person could crawl in and free the baby, shrieking from his car seat.

Liz went to comfort the woman, feeling particularly emotional. Well, of course, she chided herself. There's a life at stake. Not just any life, but a baby, like the one taking root inside of me.

Hellboy nodded with approval at Liz then told the woman, "I'll get the baby. Go."

Seeing Hellboy close up did not calm her down. Sure, he was the idol of millions, in his own head, but to a panicked woman, he was big, scary, red-skinned monster.

Unaware of what was currently terrifying the woman, Abe approached her in his polite manner. He told her, no doubt using his telepathy for calming emphasis, "Don't worry, ma'am. He'll take care of it.

Krauss followed behind Abe and added, "Come with us, please."

She looked from the red monster to the fish-man to the guy in a diving suit with gas for a head, and Liz thought the woman would faint dead away. Instead, she shrieked anew, drowning out her infant's wails. Manning gestured and two B.P.R.D. agents approached and escorted her away.

Hellboy jogged over to the van and tried the doors to see if any could be opened even in their current misshapen condition. They refused to budge. He picked the least damaged door and decided to work his way in from there. With both hands on the handle, he gave it a tug, then a second pull. Metal made a high-pitched groan as it twisted further and actually began to bend in response to Hellboy's urgent yanking. When the handle broke in his meaty paws, he grabbed the frame around the shattered window and finished the job, putting all his strength into separating the metal hinges from the car chassis itself.

A thumping sound told him the elemental was closing in on him, now that Hellboy was a stationary target. That fueled him to give it his all in one final yank. The door finally agreed to part from the car and he tossed it aside with a grunt. Carefully, with tenderness that showed how many years he had handled fragile things such as kittens, Hellboy disengaged the crying baby boy from the car seat. Making cooing noises to try and calm down the frightened child, Hellboy made an odd sight, one that actually comforted Liz. Gave her fleeting hope.

Then the root-encrusted giant foot smashed the car flat.

Hellboy wrapped his massive arms to cradle the blanket-wrapped infant and began running down the block, away from the child's mother, and away from his opponent. As he ran, the elemental crushed cars, mailboxes, newspaper vending machines, whatever was in its path, clearly indicating that it was only interested in obliterating Hellboy from the earth.

She also noticed that with each footstep, the elemental was leaving spores behind that rapidly took root through concrete, asphalt, and other surfaces. The roots flourished, powered by some nasty form of magic, and became vines or stalks followed by thickening branches blossoming with new life. If this thing walked the entire borough, Brooklyn would become the northeast's largest forest in hours.

Hellboy had seen the same thing and continued to expose himself, attracting the elemental. "Hey, Woody!" he called out, to ensure he had its attention. He then scampered over a skidding moped, the driver falling to the ground and his pizzas scattering across the street. Hellboy left the ground, still holding the baby, but leapt atop a crushed car, then another, and another, until he managed to reach a hotel, climbing up its side.

He rested briefly, catching his breath before beginning anew, now gaining handholds by using the rusted metal framework that held the vertical neon sign reading HOTEL. The baby had calmed down somewhat and whimpered, but oddly seemed comforted in the crook of Hellboy's arm. The neon lights blazed bright red, somewhat obscuring him from its view, but not fooling the creature at all.

The elemental had caught up to them and allowed a tendril to reach up and crush the T just below the pair. More verdant vegetation reached up and toward them as Hellboy watched the elemental's hands crush the E and L. There'd be no climbing back down.

It neared Hellboy as he reached the O and stepped through the metalwork, actually standing inside the round letter.

"Ready, kid?" Hellboy looked the baby right in the eyes and they seemed to connect.

The baby gurgled happily.

Then he was tossed high up into the night air. As the baby was reaching his zenith, Hellboy quickly reached into his coat pocket and reloaded Big Baby with the final shell he still carried.

Standing at the H, Hellboy calmly caught the baby, who might have giggled at the toss. Once the baby was safely in his arm, he looked at the elemental, which was nearing him with more crushing vines.

"You woke the baby up!" he yelled and then fired.

This time, the bullet struck the head and the creature actually staggered, banging into the building, crushing portions of the walls. A sound not unlike a bellow of pain was emitted from somewhere below Hellboy.

His radio crackled and Krauss instructed, *"Shoot it again! You must shoot it—in the energy ganglion!"*

He blinked and stared at the wounded thing, trying to imagine what the bubble head wanted. "The what?!"

"The head. Shoot it in the head!"

Hellboy took aim, trying to spot the ganglion through the thickening plant life that had no business on the side of a hotel. The H was entirely covered with blooming new life; a somewhat sweet fragrance wafted near him. The vines were rough but the leaves were silky, the flowers colorful and distracting.

There! Hellboy saw what Krauss was talking about. The elemental and the man with the gun made eye contact and stared at one another in silence.

"Do it!!" Krauss cried from below.

Hellboy continued to hesitate. He seemed uncertain.

He was shocked when a familiar voice spoke from the roof just above his position.

"What are you waiting for? This is what you wanted, isn't it?" It was Nuada, looking arrogant and unfazed that his creation was about to be destroyed. What was this guy made of?

Hellboy stared in wonderment, the baby cooing in his arm, the creature whimpering below him.

"Look at it," the prince continued. "The last of its race. Just like us. If you destroy it, the earth will never see its like again."

In a final act of vengeance, the creature fulfilled its instructions and reached one more time for Hellboy.

"You have more in common with us than with them," Nuada said.

"Take it! Take the shot! That's an order!!" Krauss ordered, sounding particularly shrill.

"You could be a king . . ." Nuada said. Hellboy may have had the red skin of a devil, but Nuada was the tempter now.

"Take him!" Krauss interrupted.

" . . . but then again, if you can't command, like any peasant, you must obey."

"Damn." He didn't want to be a king. He didn't want to go down in legend as the one who killed the last of a kind. He didn't want more people to lose their homes or lives because of a war they knew nothing about.

He took the shot.

The cerebral heart exploded on impact and the creature fell away from the building, the plant life withering instantly.

After seeing the last elemental perish, Hellboy looked at the innocent life in his arm and knew he had done good. He craned his neck to tell Nuada, but the prince had vanished as mysteriously as he had arrived.

While the vines and stalks that made up the elemental's body withered, the rest of the plant life it left in its wake continued to take hold and flourish. It was a final gift from a being that was from a time when the only humans who roamed the earth were probably Adam and Eve.

In fact, this section of Brooklyn more closely resembled the Garden of Eden than New York City. Insects were already taking up residence in the loamy surface while birds flocked in search of food and nest-makings.

He watched as the elemental's husk collapsed, gravity claiming it for the earth, and it settled in a heap.

The baby gurgled again and Hellboy knew it was time to head back down as well.

The elemental's death may have stopped the spread of the new life, but whatever he planted had continued its accelerated development, as blocks were swallowed up by the growth and had become a forest.

Abe and Nuala, followed by Manning, walked in astonishment, admiring the variety of trees and plants that threatened to block out the night sky. One section opened up into a gentle glade, with bright green grass and exotic flora ringing the space. Hummingbirds actually turned up, seemingly out of nowhere, and fluttered about Liz and Krauss. She smiled her first genuine, contented smile in what felt like forever.

Survivors, those who were unharmed but probably homeless now, followed them into the space, marveling at the near-instantaneous transformation. They were standing near where the elemental's head had settled and it suddenly bloomed, emitting a powerful burst of white pollen that floated gently on the air currents, a snowfall out of season, and no one complained.

"This is so beautiful," Abe said to the princess.

"It's perfect," she said, taking his hand.

Approaching sirens in the distance reminded one and all exactly how this miracle had been performed.

Minutes later, as the sirens were finally in the vicinity, Hellboy emerged from between a thick copse. He grinned at Liz, who actually smiled back at him. The others acknowledged his presence but as he drew nearer, the general public had a different reaction.

First there were stares, then whispering, then fingers were pointed. All focused on the happy baby in his arms. The child's mother spotted Hellboy and pushed through the crowd, her finger jabbing in the air; clearly she was still rattled by the near-death experience she and her son had just endured. Once clear, she demanded, "Give me that baby!"

The crowd, serene and happy in the newfound garden, turned ugly in an instant. The woman was backed by a fat, unshaven man in a wife-beater and jeans, work boots splattered in mud. He was carrying a baseball bat and was now waving it menacingly at Hellboy, who couldn't believe his eyes.

"You damn freak!"

Freak? *Moi?* he thought, but wisely didn't say it out loud. Instead, he couldn't understand how rescuing a bunch of hoity-toity people from the tooth fairies just a few days ago was any different than rescuing a baby and saving them all from an elemental that could have as easily stepped on them as provided them with this wonder. He didn't get it.

"The baby's fine," he said, moving toward the woman to gently transfer the kid.

Instead, an authoritative voice added to the night's tension, if that were even possible.

"Put the baby down, and put your hands in the air. Now!"

A uniformed policeman had made his way through the forest and found them in the meadow. His gun was gripped in the traditional pose and his feet were spread apart, ready to fire. He wasn't here to serve or protect, but threaten and bellow.

Great.

Where the hell was Manning when he needed him, Hellboy wondered. Manning was better at this nonsense than he was.

Fresh lights broke through the streets, the powerful lamps attached to television cameras, and now that the threat was over, the air was once more filling with the whirring noise of helicopter engines. After all, it wasn't every night a portion of Brooklyn engaged in a dramatic form of urban renewal. He glanced up and counted three helicopters but heard more than that filling the air like so many insects.

The woman finally noticed that Hellboy wasn't moving so she rushed forward and grabbed the baby from his grasp. The infant made some unidentifiable noises, but they were not happy ones. Heck, maybe he was finally figuring out what had happened or, more likely, the mom made him nuts.

She was certainly having that effect on Hellboy. Now if only the cop would relax.

"I saved him," Hellboy said defensively.

The crowd seemed to have an entirely different opinion and they were sounding pretty grumpy. The guy with the baseball bat daringly spit in his direction, the spittle landing on his coat.

That did it. Now the crowd all wanted to have a piece of him and he was far enough from the others that they couldn't come to his aid. No doubt seeing Krauss or Abe would have only enraged them further.

Fortunately, more police had arrived and they switched from threatening his life to crowd control, reining in the mob before it turned into a full-scale riot.

"Hand in the air," the cop insisted. "Up—up . . ."

Seeing no choice, Hellboy slowly raised both hands into the air. He had hoped simple cooperation would calm everything down. Instead, one of the people spotted the great stone ring around his right forearm and panicked.

"He has a weapon in his hand!"

"That *is* his hand!"

It was Liz. She wormed her way through the crowd to stand near Hellboy and confronted the police and the nearest crazy people. He noted she looked damned uncomfortable but he was thrilled at how brave she was, exposing herself to protect him.

Her normal presence and the simplicity of her words caused everything to pause for just a moment.

"Miss—stay back from him. For your own safety," an officer said, clearly not getting the memo about the B.P.R.D.

Liz reached over and took the policeman's hand in her own, meeting his eyes. The act made him lower his arm, the gun no longer pointing at Hellboy. The crowd also made a surprised collective sound.

"He was trying to help, don't you see? He was just trying to help," she continued.

The news media were enthralled by the sudden drama. Digital cameras and television models were all at work, flashing away, and she blinked at every flash. A dozen arms waved camera phones in her direction as well.

"That's all we do—that's all we've done all these years. Help you—*you!*"

He was moved by her words, but clearly the crowd was not, as a stone, newly risen from the depths, became a projectile, landing on his forehead. Yeah, that was going to leave another mark.

The stone cut his skin and the dark blood oozing from the wound shimmered in the cooler air. The mob was already freaked out and just seeing a glimpse of it made them crazy. Wisely, the cops sensed the change in mood and instinctively interposed themselves between the B.P.R.D. agents and the general public.

Liz stood there, angry and hurt. Her hands flexed open and closed, tiny flickering blue flames enveloped her fingers. She reached out and took Hellboy's hand, squeezing it once, and then she seemed to relax. The flame from her other hand began to snake its way around her until she was encased in shimmering fire, ready to burn the crowd.

Instead, Red leaned his head close to hers and whispered in a very hurt tone, "No—no. Let's go home."

CHAPTER FOURTEEN

The ride from Brooklyn to New Jersey was handled thanks to Manning actually doing his job. He flashed his credentials and arranged a police escort while Liz and Hellboy were confronted by the mob. Just before things turned truly ugly, the cops' radios came to life and ordered them to escort the agents out of the forest and back to the city. It was tough as the mob followed, tossing additional stones and insults. The newly grown grass was trampled and the new Eden was already being spoiled from dropped beer bottles, wrappers, and even urine.

Still, the cops made certain nothing else went wrong and as they emerged from the undergrowth, a police transport was awaiting them with motorcycle officers in front and back. Other police and rescue workers tended to the damaged buildings, debris-filled streets, and countless wrecked cars littering the area. It was already being declared a disaster area by the governor and every channel, both broadcast and cable, seemed to be beaming live footage, trying to connect the new trees growing in Brooklyn with the exposure of Hellboy and the other "freaks."

Manning, Abe, Nuala, Krauss, Liz, and Hellboy were allowed access to the transport, a modified bus; but several officers were also assigned, riot guns in hand, to make certain nothing else went wrong. The minute the door sealed shut, the convoy moved out, taking a circuitous route considering the Brooklyn Bridge itself had been shut. From the communications center, Manning was talking with New Jersey police to make certain there'd be no territorial nonsense when they reached the border. He then contacted the B.P.R.D. headquarters to dispatch several agents to keep an eye on the Jersey troopers. He also asked that quarters for Nuala be set up and to open the kitchen so the exhausted team could have a meal.

Satisfied things were well in hand, Manning put down his cell phone, turned to Krauss and asked, "Can someone tell me what the hell just happened? I mean, first we go looking for the Troll Market and the next thing I know, the Jolly Green Giant arrives and turns Brooklyn into a new Central Park."

Krauss turned his helmeted head to look at Hellboy and Liz, who were huddled together, neither looking up. For a change, they seemed content to let him actually lead.

"Well, Dr. Manning, we appear to be at war."

"War? Did you say war?" Manning spluttered. "With whom?"

"The Children of the Earth," Krauss answered. "Long ago, when man and elf more overtly shared the planet, their differences led to a conflict, one that nearly ended man's life on the planet. Nuada Silverlance, our princess's brother, wants to resume that conflict with mankind and is attempting to resurrect a terrible weapon, the Golden Army."

Manning turned to the princess, who was seated quietly next to Abe, and didn't they look chummy?

"Can't you stop him?"

She sadly shook her head no and remained silent for a bit. Manning's stare, though, compelled her to say something.

"He killed our father. There's nothing I can do to stop him, except keep him from finding the final piece."

"Final piece? Of what? Elf pie?"

"A little courtesy, Dr. Manning," Krauss said mildly. "She is an ally and now a guest of the Bureau. She is royalty."

"The prince is attempting to recreate a crown that was separated as part of a pact reached between my father and mankind."

"When was this?"

"So long ago, I don't know if your kind kept calendars," she said.

"You're looking very well preserved," Manning said snidely.

Ignoring the comment, Krauss continued. "Her father was King Balor, a name we have inscribed in several tomes. He recognized that the Golden Army was too terrible a weapon to leave active and forged a truce. The crown that gave the wearer control over the army was broken into three. Apparently, Prince Nuada has felt the time has come to resume the conflict and obtained the piece given to man for safekeeping. By killing his father, he now possesses two of the three pieces."

"And if he gets that third piece?"

"Then an unstoppable army will circle the globe and, being forged from goblin fires, will likely withstand whatever is thrown at it."

Manning paused, eyes wide, swallowing deeply, and absorbed all this.

"How did he declare this war?"

"By sending that elemental to attack Agent Hellboy without regard for the people around him. You must understand, Doctor, he feels he is fighting for his race's survival."

"What race are you?" Manning asked the princess.

"Under my father, he managed to unite the Children of the Earth," she explained. "All of us, the trolls, goblins, orcs, and other races that are but the stuff of your children's fairy tales, are real. They abided by the peace my father created and were willing to retreat further and further from man's domination of the planet. My brother felt we were on the verge of being extinct."

Liz pressed a compress to Hellboy's head and Abe sat in silence, merely holding Nuala's hand. The princess appeared sad, perhaps for the loss of the elemental, or more likely, the estrangement from her brother. The mere thought of Nuada reminded them all that he was free and mobile. His declaration of war against mankind had not yet been received by mankind. After all, unlike the world below, humanity was not quite unified. As a result, only those aware of the impending battle to come were in a position to stop it.

Liz doubted the B.P.R.D. were up to the task right now. They needed rest, intelligence, and then a plan. While Hellboy might want to go out guns blazing, it would not protect humanity. Krauss might know something that could turn the tide, but she had her doubts. Abe would fight but be among the first to fall, she feared.

Her hand rubbing her belly, she thought she'd be right behind him. Sure, she could go nova and take out a horde or two, but she was just one freak against an army that couldn't be counted.

She looked at the princess, felt some sympathy for her plight, but also wondered what else she knew. Could she possess an insight into her twin that could help stop a terrible war from even starting?

"Do we tell Washington?" Manning asked after another long, uncomfortable silence.

"I would think not, Dr. Manning," Krauss said. "They will escalate this without taking the time to understand what we're dealing with. Our work is usually met with skepticism and we're likely going to waste time trying to convince them otherwise. No, I think it best we try and find Nuada and dissuade him from this reckless course."

Nuala shook her head in silence, telling them that the efforts were likely to be fruitless.

Liz saw the gesture and any hope she had of surviving this battle grew dimmer.

Once they were back at headquarters, Manning had Nuala escorted to a room while Abe refreshed himself in his tank. Liz took Hellboy by the hand and led him back to their quarters, bypassing the infirmary. As they entered the room, she looked wistfully at the hole that had finally had some covering added so they once more had privacy. Several of the cats emerged as they settled in the bathroom and Hellboy cooed at them weakly. He clearly didn't want to talk, turning the televisions on, set as usual to Turner Classic Movies and another film channel.

She ignored the flickering images of Elsa Lanchester lying on the lab table, still wrapped like a mummy, and of Virginia Mayo arguing with Jimmy Cagney. Instead of sitting beside him, she checked the wastebasket to make certain the cleaning staff had been through the room. A wave of relief flooded her that that was going to be one topic they could avoid today.

A steward arrived with several white cartons of takeout Chinese food, something Hellboy had requested in the vehicle. No one wanted to argue so Manning had had Marble make the call. They'd eat once she had finished tending to his wound. Her efforts were good enough, ever since she had applied pressure en route from Brooklyn. The bleeding had stopped but now she used hydrogen peroxide and other unguents to clean and dress the wound and other scrapes he had collected over the last few hours. It amazed her that it had only been a day and they had found the fabled Troll Market and then mowed down the last of a race of elementals. They had left wreckage everywhere they went, opposite the elemental's path, which partially restored the borough to a long-lost luster.

And Hellboy had endured so much, including the hatred of the uninformed. Still, he had rescued the infant and stopped the elemental from hurting even more innocent people—the same ones who had then turned on him. "You did a good job out there," she told him.

"I did, uh? Then tell me, why don't I feel good? I killed that . . . thing . . . and for what? They don't like me—didn't you notice?"

Together, they slowly walked from the bathroom and sat down to eat their meal—breakfast or brunch or late supper, whatever it could be called. Liz only put a little food on her paper plate, not feeling hungry, and she couldn't be certain if it was the exhaustion or the notion of Chinese food at this hour.

He filled his plate high with pork fried rice, spicy Szechwan chicken, and topped it with an egg roll. Before digging in, he flipped the channels, giving up on the old movies and watching the endless news coverage of the events they had actually experienced.

Shots of the carnage were evident along with a dark-suited talking head speculating as to what the elemental might have been. Hellboy kept everything on mute and stared at his food, clearly troubled.

Liz felt even more troubled. He got what he asked for. She didn't ask for what had happened to her.

"Red, I am leaving—for a while."

She gave him a weak smile, trying to be brave about this. He just stared at her, a lost little boy all of a sudden.

"What do you mean?"

Liz fiddled with her hands, nervous and unable to put her feelings into words, not without bringing up the baby—a baby she was uncertain about. It was tearing her up inside and all she wanted was to find a room where she could sit and collect her thoughts. Someplace safe, someplace far from Nuada's mad war.

"I need time to think," was all she could manage.

"Where? About what?" Hellboy ignored the televisions, his food, and the cats piled around his feet. Instead, he focused solely on her and it gave her unexpected strength.

"Things. Us."

Hellboy blinked at that. "Can't you think right in here? I'll be quiet. Get rid of the cats."

"It's not the cats," she said.

"Then what? Tell me—please."

"I made a mistake—a big mistake."

Both seemed to need to take a breath and they each glanced at the screens. It was an ill-conceived move since at that moment, the footage being shown was Liz touching Hellboy and in large letters underneath, the network declared: "Outrage."

She quickly turned to him, looking right into his eyes, feeling ready to bolt and unwilling to just abandon him.

"Why are you with me, Red?" she asked in a soft voice. "I need to know. Do you need *everybody* to like you?"

She moved closer to his face.

"Or am I enough?"

"You," he began but fell silent as she leaned in and kissed him on the forehead, not far from where she had patched him up.

"Don't answer me now. Just think about it."

She got up and slowly walked out of the room, once more Hellboy's sole domain. He absently hit the remote control and one monitor switched back to *Bride of Frankenstein* just in time for Boris Karloff to reach for the master lever and say, "We belong dead."

In the library, Abe had swum for a bit, eaten, and felt substantially better. The buoyancy of the water seemed to match his mood. Yes, the world was in imminent danger and people were blissfully unaware. But that seemed smaller, more manageable than it would have a day or two earlier.

First there was Krauss, who kept him intellectually stimulated, and then he met Nuala, who awakened feelings he had never thought he could possess. She filled him with light, with the sense that anything was possible. After she had refreshed herself, she asked to be brought to him and she watched happily as he gracefully moved through his tank.

Odd, he had never thought of the tank as confining before, but now it seemed insufficiently small.

He finished his swim and quickly climbed out of the tank, emerging on the library's upper level. Carefully, he reached into a case that was specially molded and contained microcircuits that monitored the conditions within. Once the hinged top flipped open, he removed two sclera lenses and with some difficulty and discomfort, fitted them over his eyes. He was glad no one watched him do this or saw the way he contorted his face during the process.

When they had settled into place, he blinked several times to make certain and then picked up his gill hydrator, a handheld, pressurized water injector, and used it to ready his body for a prolonged time away from the tank. He felt the rush of water seep into his gills and allow him to take several deep breaths.

Once the water had stopped flowing, he replaced the device and concentrated on his surroundings. Nuala's voice drifted up from the lower level and he smiled in recognition of the words. He peered over the railing and watched her reading from a volume, held carefully in her hands. Where Krauss was filled with insight into the paranormal, Nuala seemed to have her own view into the soul.

> *Be near me when my light is low,*
> *When the blood creeps, and the nerves prick*
> *And tingle; and the heart is sick,*
> *And all the wheels of Being . . .*

He walked down the staircase, quietly, and when she was done, he said, "Tennyson. 'In Memoriam.'"

The princess spun around, surprised she had been observed, but she smiled shyly at him and then more broadly as he neared.

"A beautiful poem," Abe continued. "The last stanza is so moving."

He neared her and drank in her presence, her sweet scent. "You're safe here. Nothing will harm you," he assured her.

With a sad shake of her head, she said, "My brother will find me. He always does."

"How could he? Our location is a highly classified secret."

"I know of it now, which means he does, too. We are twins."

She shelved the book, her fingers tracing the old, worn spine. "Even as children, a link bound us, one to the other. It's something I cannot explain."

"No need," Abe said, taking her hand once more and leading her toward the center of the library. The mere touch of her soft skin thrilled him beyond experience.

"The danger with him, you see, is that he believes that this is a just war."

Her words disturbed him, threatened to spoil the magical mood. But of course, she was right and he was being silly. Maybe it was time to start planning to stop the war or defend humanity. Both seemed equally impossible.

"We will care for you here."

They paused and she turned to face him, her brown eyes penetrating his own. She looked deeply and appraisingly before saying another word. Finally, she concluded, "You look different."

"Oh, do I? Perhaps my hair . . . ?"

She smiled at the joke, as another thrill ran through him from head to toe. He rarely made jokes and to have her appreciate it was beyond his expectation. Abe honestly had no idea what to expect from her or what they could possibly expect together, but he knew in his heart he wanted to be with her until the end of time. Her twin brother might see to it, though, that the end was imminent.

"It's your eyes," she finally realized. "I can see your eyes."

He nodded and was about to explain about the lenses when he spotted her crystal scroll unfurled atop a worktable. Together, they walked over to it and studied the parchment.

"Is that a map?"

She nodded, concurring with the obvious. It was a piece of brittle, worn parchment, with dyed inks inscribing a map of some unfamiliar terrain. The map lacked recognizable landmarks or a scale, so he had no way of knowing if they were seeing a continent, an island, or a smaller space.

"It was in the cylinder," the princess explained. "A global chart—but there are no coordinates."

"Perhaps there's a watermark?" Gingerly, Abe lifted the parchment and held it before one of the floor lamps. The light proved the paper opaque but no obvious symbols or marks appeared to him.

As he lowered it, Abe noticed she was studying him, eyeing him as if for the first time. Despite all the rushing around they had done, clearly smitten with one another, and having been in intimate danger, this was the first time they had been alone and could speak freely with one another. He thought he should be nervous but found he wasn't. They'd already faced near-death together, and that shared experience seemed to seal whatever instant bond had been forged on that first encounter. It was the stuff of poetry and mythology, Abe considered.

"You were very brave, vouching for me," she told him. "How do you know I'm not the enemy, bringing me here?"

He looked back, studying her beauty, the depth behind her eyes. It was simple. "It's as you were saying, just now. From intuition . . . maybe . . . a link . . ."

Abe gazed more deeply into her eyes, his telepathic powers augmenting the look, and he felt welcomed within her mind.

"Normally, I am able to read others quite quickly," he said with hesitation. "But—I've never met anyone like you."

"Nor I like you."

The shower area of the B.P.R.D. locker room was roomier than the shower in his bathroom, so it was not unusual for Hellboy to be seen washing up where the rest of the agents congregated. He was there, letting the water run as hot and hard as possible, lost in thought.

Hellboy popped open a beer and drank deeply, ignoring the spray of water that diluted its potency.

He didn't care.

He reviewed the last hour in his mind. Then the last day. Then the last week. He was seeking clues, things said or not said, things he should have picked up on to better comprehend why Liz was leaving. It had been coming since the arguments started and she had grown moody. He always gave her space when she got moody, knowing all the demons she allowed to fester in her mind. Still, there was moody and there was *moody* and she had most certainly grown the latter and he still had no idea why.

Realizing he was just standing there uselessly, he finally turned off the spray and let himself drip a bit before toweling down. No one else was around which was fine by him. Maybe after this he'd blow off steam at the target range. After all, a new supply of Manning targets had arrived and he wanted to see how small a caliber he could shoot and still hit the bull's-eye, right between his eyes.

Finished, he dropped the towel and walked over to the locker where his clothes and a fresh six-pack of beer awaited him. He finished one can as he slowly put his fresh clothes on.

He seemed entirely oblivious to the arrival of Johann Krauss, who silently opened a locker and began organizing his own belongings. They ignored one another until Krauss's belt fell noisily to the bench, knocking his colleague's deodorant stick to the tiled floor.

"Hey! Watch it, pal!" Hellboy snapped, his voice echoing in the locker room.

Krauss turned and nodded, gazing at Hellboy, although it was hard to tell as the gas within the transparent bubble swirled about.

"Agent . . . I know you don't like me."

Noncommittal, Hellboy opened a beer and drank. "Mmh."

"But—you could lose your badge."

Hellboy closed his locker and walked away, not at all interested in the conversation. He did say over his shoulder, "Never got one. Kept asking though."

"You should concentrate. Follow protocol. Be focused." Now Krauss was sounding like a schoolmarm. Or worse, Manning.

Hellboy paused, crushed the empty can in his hand and fiddled with it as he replied. "That word. With your accent. *Fockused.* I wouldn't use it much."

The senior agent shook his head slowly. He seemed disappointed in Hellboy. Great, another one to add to the list. Hellboy wondered when Abe was going to abandon him, too.

"It's all a joke to you, isn't it??"

He began to walk to the locker-room door, done with the conversation. That was the plan, until Krauss spoke the magic words.

"I knew Professor Broom."

Okay, that was enough. Pop psychology was one thing, but this felt like a blow below the belt. "You didn't . . ." he started but was cut off.

"In my human form," Krauss insisted. He even sounded sincere. "We served together . . . the Budapest incident in '59."

There was something that had happened in Budapest and 1959 felt right but could Krauss have been there? Was he really that long-lived? Well, the fish-man was, so why not a bag of gas?

"Stop it." He couldn't stop the hurt and the anger from his words but he wanted to control himself. He wanted to show he was better than that. He had to prove it to *her*.

"Even then, you were foremost in his mind. He was worried about your future —what would happen to you after he . . ."

"If I were you, Gasbag . . . I would shut up, right now." Hellboy shrugged off Krauss's attempt at male bonding.

"Or? What? Are you threatening me?"

Another shrug. He wanted to be good but damn, Krauss was pressing his buttons. Of course, he had so many buttons these days.

"Because I think I can take you."

Well, that was interesting and unexpected. Brawling with the boss, though, wouldn't go over well, with anyone. Starting with and not exclusively limited to Liz. Still, he couldn't let it go unchallenged. "Excuse me?"

He walked back into the room, closer to Krauss, who stood his ground by the still-open locker. "I couldn't hear from over there."

"You heard me."

Hellboy continued to stare.

"You're strong. I'll give you that."

"Give me?" Hellboy asked, incredulous as all get out.

"But you have a fatal flaw," the other agent said, once more in teaching mode.

"I wanna hear it."

"No, you don't," Krauss insisted. "You can't take criticism."

"Try me."

"Can't take it . . ." the Austrian said emphatically.

"Try me," Hellboy offered, feeling his blood rushing throughout his body. He resisted raising his fist. "What is my flaw??"

"Your temperament. It gets the best of you. Makes you weak and vul . . ."

That did it. Hellboy swung his right arm in an arc that allowed the larger and heavier stone ring that was his forearm to smash into the helmet. To his utter shock, the glass shattered. He had always assumed that they'd have some space-age material to make sure that this wouldn't happen.

Then again, he realized, he made an ass out of me, skip the you.

The gas speedily escaped the now-open containment suit, which collapsed to the floor, a heap of canvas and nozzles. A hissing sound filled the area, punctuating the horror of his action.

"Aw, crap," Hellboy said. Looking around at the mist, which seemed to mingle with the remnants of water vapor from his long shower, he was on the verge of panic. He leaned over the now-empty suit. "Johann, hang on, pal. Johann? Johann?"

So focused was he on the outfit that he did not notice the gas coalesce, and a tendril reached out and made contact with the nearest bank of metal lockers. Instants later, the beige doors flapped back and forth, catching Hellboy unaware. He found himself stuck between two lockers, their doors rapidly opening and closing, smacking him repeatedly in the face. The force of each blow was enough to leave imprints in Hellboy's crimson skin, showing exactly where the combination lock, handle, and unit number were located.

Then, the beating slowed and a voice echoed from deep within the empty spaces.

"See? Your temper . . . makes you sloppy."

Krauss moved away, locker doors slamming shut to indicate his passage out of the locker room. Hellboy watched glumly, and then rubbed his raw, battered face. He briefly flashed on how tenderly Liz had dressed the wound just a short while ago and now there was no one to help him.

Liz had left him.

He sat on the floor of the locker room, thankful no one else had dared enter. He sat alone, frustrated and extremely sad.

As for Krauss, he had just one word for his superior.

"Glasshole."

CHAPTER FIFTEEN

Hellboy didn't have the first notion of how they were going to find and stop Nuada and his war. He did know it was serious and that all life on earth was being threatened. Deep down, the younger boy he once was quivered in fear.

Right now, though, he didn't care.

Liz had left, he'd been one-upped by Krauss, and the world hated him after loving him for just about his promised fifteen minutes. He was feeling all alone, missing Broom harder than he had in weeks, and felt adrift.

Which all went to explain how he wound up wandering the cold steel corridors of B.P.R.D. headquarters, carrying two six-packs of beer and feeling totally lost. Sipping from one can, he paused to swallow and heard music. It wasn't the classical stuff Abe normally played. In fact, it was sounding mournful and full of angst. Worse, it sounded like Barry Manilow.

That actually piqued his curiosity, which had been napping the last day or so. He walked closer to the door and entered the sumptuously appointed library. Instantly, its smells made him think of happier times: when Broom had tried to teach him chess or he had found some favorite childhood books awaiting him on one particular shelf. There were many late-night games and discussions held here; this was a sanctuary.

Therefore, the notion that he could hear 1970s pop crap irritated him.

He looked toward the glass walls that held back thousands of gallons of carefully treated water and saw Abe out of his aquatic home, standing by the wall, listening to the music.

Abe seemed serenely lost in thought, causing Hellboy to gape in wonderment. He knew the fish-man had fallen for the princess and he had to admit, she was a looker, but what would send him to listening to something so melancholy if he had just found true love?

He must have been emanating some powerful emotions because Abe picked up on them across the distance and turned to face his long-time friend and confidant. The amphibian looked at Hellboy and nodded in welcome.

"Ah, hello, Red. You're up late."

Hellboy noticed all the beer he had been drinking had finally reached the point where he was slightly buzzed, taking the edge off his own roiling emotions. In fact, he was feeling pretty damned sociable all of a sudden. "What are you listening to?"

"It was er, urm, Vivaldi," Abe said. It came out quickly and he was badly covering up what they both knew to be the truth. "*Il cimento dell'armonia*. I particularly admire that last passage . . ."

As Abe yammered on, Hellboy walked over to the stereo system and popped out the compact disc. He took one glance to confirm his hearing. Vivaldi would never have been included on anything called *Greatest Love Songs*.

"Oh. *That*. Yes . . ." Hellboy agreed, giving his friend a goofy grin. The secret was safe between them. Still, he had to bust Abe's ass just a bit.

"*Greatest Love Songs*. You, the brains of the operation," he snickered and settled into an easy chair, dropping the two six-packs, allowing the deep pile carpet to cushion the sound.

Abe moved closer, ready to pour out his soul, and he was ready to listen. After all, it gave Hellboy something to think about rather than his own sorry state of affairs. On the other hand, he had limited tolerance for hearing about anyone's greatest love right now, Abe's or Barry Manilow's.

"It's her," Abe insisted. "She's changed me, Red! I never knew! Until I saw her!"

"The princess?" Hellboy asked even though he damned well knew the answer. Abe foolishly nodded his head, following it with the first of several heavy sighs.

"C'mon, Abe. You fell for the princess?"

"She's like me, a creature from another world. What am I? A made-up name for a thing found in a jar." Abe was gesturing inside his tank and Hellboy wasn't entirely certain what he was trying to convey, but he did know that what Abe was spouting was a far stretch from the truth.

"Jeez, you need to get out more," he advised his friend, who seemed to blithely ignore him.

"She's alone in the world. And I want to help her. I need to care for her."

Reaching for the six-pack, he grabbed a can, ripped it free from the plastic holder, and thrust it out. "You're in love," Hellboy confirmed. "Have a beer." He then picked up his can and took a gulp in salute.

Abe, though, refused to take the offering. Folding his arms in defiance, he informed Hellboy, "My body is a temple."

Hellboy nodded in confirmation then added without a pause, "Mine's an amusement park."

The beer remained in midair, the beefy hand offering it rock steady, and Abe kept staring at it. Never before had Hellboy felt like a devil tempting some poor innocent schmuck. If he was going to drink, he decided he'd rather not do it alone. That was just too sad and pathetic.

"No—no . . . the glandular balance of . . . " Abe protested.
"Shut up and drink."

Abe finally succumbed and withdrew the can from Hellboy's hand. He ran his hands over it, as if studying it for the first time. Hellboy went back to the stereo and picked up the disc. He opened the tray and let it fall into place.

"What track?"

"Eight."

Before acquiescing, Hellboy studied the song titles imprinted atop the disc and asked, " 'Can't Smile without You'?" He then shot Abe a sickening look, unable to believe they were going to play the track a second time. Maybe being lovesick made the amphibian addlebrained.

"I know."

Well, in for a penny, in for a pound, Hellboy mused as he closed the tray and activated the track. As the 1978 number-one pop hit began to resound from the surround-sound speakers, Hellboy mused that the 1970s were not a particularly good decade for music. Still, this seemed to fit Abe's mood and maybe his own. Damn, he missed Liz so much it hurt. And when you're hurt, you anesthetize the wound.

"I'll need a beer, too," he said, reaching for a fresh can.

Finally, Abe's well-manicured fingers popped the top and the sound never sounded better. As he sampled the aroma of malt and hops, foamy suds exploded from the top, running down the sides and dripping onto the carpet, soaking in, turning the surface into a deeper shade of red, almost black. All Hellboy saw was wasted suds.

"Oh, my God . . ." Abe cried out and held the can up, slurping up the sliding foam and then taking a tentative sip. He seemed to quiver for a second then settled down. Once more, he studied the can as if it were some paranormal artifact.

You know I can't smile without you
I can't smile without you
I can't laugh and I can't sing
I'm finding it hard to do anything
You see I feel sad when you're sad . . .

Barry sang and Abe listened intently, daring to take baby sips. He then looked right at Hellboy, gestured with the hand holding the beer and said, "See? I love this song and I can't smile or cry . . ."

Hellboy cocked his head quizzically.

"I have no tear ducts," Abe explained and to Hellboy *that* was sad.

As Barry warbled through the song, Hellboy looked around the room and finally voiced his feelings, something he didn't do to people other than Abe and Liz. Since Liz was driving him to feel this way, he had only Abe now.

"I miss my father. He'd know what to tell you—us."

Abe finally took a seat near Hellboy, his sips now longer ones. The silence between them was sad, yes, but it was also a comfortable silence between old friends. Their guards were down and they finally allowed themselves to relax. Shortly, one, then the other—neither realized who went first—began to hum along with the music. When the next chorus began, they both sang along, softly and without feeling at all self-conscious. At the end of the chorus, they revved it up and were suddenly belting it out at the top of their lungs, letting their emotions intertwine with the saccharine lyrics. Maybe Chris Arnold, David Martin, and Geoff Morrow, the writers behind the much-covered hit, knew something about the inner workings of the broken heart after all.

————————

Their voices carried beyond the door and down the halls. The construction of the corridors allowed the sound to travel and the late hour meant there was little noise to compete with it.

As a result, B.P.R.D. agents on duty nodded in recognition, one or two of them even humming along.

The sound of the two men singing reached as far as Hellboy's own quarters. Within, Liz sat, almost done gathering up her things. She'd be gone in the morning but right now, she put down the sweater in her hands and listened. A slow, sad smile crossed her face.

The singing also gave Johann Krauss pause. He heard the sounds and it took him some time to identify them, parsing the off-tune men from the distinctive, melodious voice of Barry Manilow. The great Manilow would have made Krauss smile but he no longer possessed a physical body. Instead, he stopped work, putting the piece of 150-grit sandpaper on his worktable. It had taken him hours to unpack his prized possession, a grand victorian dollhouse, and set it up to his specifications. He'd barely had time to acclimate to his new quarters since arriving from Washington and he forced himself to do so now, to process the experiences just completed.

When he had been summoned from Washington, he had made certain that this would be accompanying him and agents had worked overtime to ready the space. In his gloved hand was an exquisite miniature dining room table. He'd been sanding it to perfection when he paused and now he examined it and decided it was complete. He turned around and gently placed it within the dining room and then reached beside the house for the *coffret*. He withdrew from it a velvet pouch, worn with age, and embroidered with the letter K. Weighing it in his palm, Krauss carefully removed a small photograph, brown with age. He gazed at the headshot of a beautiful woman, her hairstyle denoting the Victorian age.

He too began to hum with the music.

The princess was in her own quarters, trying to sleep. The music, alien to her, captured her attention and kept her awake. Not that sleep was at all on the horizon. Too much had happened, too much was going to happen to allow her to use this respite for sleep. Instead, wearing one of Liz's nightgowns, she tossed and turned, unable to find a comfortable position. Everyone had been so nice, so welcoming, that she despaired for their fates, knowing the path her twin put them all on could only mean death and destruction. She closed her eyes and shuddered, shaking the mattress.

Then, the eyes snapped open and a new sensation flooded her awareness.

"No—no. He's here . . ."

CHAPTER SIXTEEN

Outside B.P.R.D. headquarters, Nuada's finely attuned senses managed to hear the music. While the high-tech security system kept the unwanted out, it was still porous enough for music to escape.

It paled in comparison with the great songs of love and loss that the troll bards had written when he was but a lad.

The prince stood listening as he carefully, lovingly, wiped his sword clean, using fabric torn from one of the two dead guards at his feet. Their blood seeped into the dirt road, blending in with its surroundings, much like the facility.

Finished, he placed the sword back in its hilt and then bent low to caress the head of the panting guard dog that obediently sat still.

"Good dog," he offered.

The twin six-packs had been emptied but Hellboy did not at all feel done for the night. Abe seemed to agree so they left the library to liberate a fresh six-pack from Hellboy's well-stocked fridge.

As they entered the room, Abe saw that Liz was finally asleep and he lingered near the door so as not to wake her. He could not help but notice the packed bags and her clear intention of running from the B.P.R.D., Red, and her own problems—once more. She was accompanied by several of the cats, who also slept, positioned around her like protectors.

Red, though, gave her a glance and decided his need for beer outweighed her need for silence.

"This—this is all right. Quite delicious. And full of nutrients," Abe said, clearly feeling the alcohol's effects. He had rarely drunk anything like beer or wine so his body was unused to its effects and he seemed to have a little difficulty standing straight.

"And it's light," Hellboy added cheerily.

The beer now safely nestled in his left arm, Hellboy paused at the bed, watching Liz sleep. She was so beautiful at rest, so at peace with a world that had hurt her. Seeing her stirred unhappy feelings anew, causing him to frown.

"Look at her," he began. In a quiet voice, he added, "She's it, Abe. She's it. She's my whole wide w—you know?"

He paused and studied her some more, breathing heavily through his nostrils.

"I would give my life—for her—but she also wants me to do the dishes!"

Abe came closer and leaned in to Hellboy, the beer breath preceding him. "I—I would die and do the dishes," he declared.

"Shh. You're going to wake her."

To stay silent, Abe raised a fresh beer and took a sip.

"Why? Why is she mad at me? It's not the room—I know—it's something else."

Neither realized, and Abe was too inebriated to sense, that Liz had been awoken by the drunken stumbling. She willed herself to remain still, but opened her eyes to force herself to remain awake, and to listen.

"Ask her, then," Abe insisted.

Hellboy staggered a bit, nearly teetering onto the bed and crushing his lover. He righted himself and waved Abe off. "No," he said. "Listen, Abe, when a woman's mad about *something* and she really is mad about *something else*—you can't ask—'cause then she gets angrier 'cause you had to ask. So— you have to find out . . ."

She smiled at that, pleased he had learned that much.

Back in her regular blue robes, Nuala hurriedly left her quarters and sought Abe in the library. She was initially disappointed to open the door and see the empty tank. She then noticed the discarded beer cans, half of them crushed flat, and the stereo still on. That meant Abe was around somewhere but she was unsure of how to contact him.

Her breathing was rapid and she could feel her pulse quicken as she knew she had very little time to work.

First things first. She withdrew the metal cylinder from her belt and popped it open, carelessly withdrawing the map. Without a final glance, she walked over to the fireplace, still glowing with flames that were working through a high pile of logs, and threw the map within. Instantly, the aged parchment caught flame and was blackened within instants. Once it was ashes, she tossed in the cylinder, letting the heat begin to melt and ruin it, making it a useless vessel.

Then, she crossed to a familiar bookcase and carefully removed the final piece of the golden crown and slipped it within the pages of the Tennyson book she had grown fond of. In fact, she placed it right where "In Memoriam" began.

No sooner did the book slip back into its place than the door to the library opened anew and her breath caught.

Walking in was her brother, casually, as if he had been here all along.

"Sister."

Rather than walk to her, as she expected, he went right for the fireplace, explaining as he crossed the vast room. "Very quick of you. Alas, the parchment was of no importance. The cylinder, however, is very interesting."

Without fear of burning, he reached in and withdrew the white-hot cylinder. He hefted it away from the hungry flames and walked over to the desk and rolled it one complete turn. The heated metal charred an impression into the leather desk covering, symbols and images taking shapes in shades of brown and black.

"Now we know where we need to go," he said, smiling to himself. Nuala remained near the bookcase, afraid to give away her secret. "As for the crown piece I know it's here. I can read that much. In here—one of these books."

Tossing the cooling metal object aside, he took several swift strides toward a nearby bookcase and began grabbing books, one at a time, and judging them wanting, let them fall haphazardly to the floor. Spines split, pages were bent, and at no time did he seem to care. Intent as he was on his mission, she feared he'd find it and then the world would be forever doomed.

Then her eyes fell on an alarm panel.

Abe and Hellboy remained standing by the bed, all thought of silence forgotten. Both gazed at Liz, who struggled to remain still. They sipped at their beers and were seemingly lost in their own thoughts.

"I can tell you . . . I know."

Liz shuddered a bit but neither noticed. She was willing the drunk fish-man to remain quiet, leaving her with some shred of dignity, some sense she still had control of the situation.

"Know what?" Hellboy inquired.

"What's going on with Liz."

That caught his attention and he took a step closer to Abe, suddenly appearing like a menace, not a friend.

"You do?"

Abe looked at him, at the neediness in his eyes. The alcohol would loosen those fish lips, Liz feared.

"Red," he began.

She finally couldn't risk to remain silent or still. She shot up, causing both men to take a surprised step back. Her look implored Abe to pick up on her need for privacy.

"Abe—no . . ."

Surprisingly, Abe cut her off. "I'm sorry. He has to know."

Hellboy asked, "Know what?" and it was clear he was losing patience, as the alcohol had lowered his meager internal governor.

Liz looked at Abe, who said, while keeping his eyes on her. "Red—you're going to be a . . ."

The shrill alarm klaxon drowned out the final words.

Thankfully, Liz thought, as she leapt from bed and went for her clothes, scattering the kittens. Whatever was the cause, it was a lifesaver and she was going to give it a big, sloppy kiss.

Then smack Abe.

CHAPTER SEVENTEEN

B.P.R.D. agents filled the corridors, scrambling to their assigned posts. Those who had been awoken were still tucking in shirts or adjusting earpieces, but they were all armed and ready. This alarm rarely rung out so they knew it was something to respect.

As a result, the trio had difficulty making their way from the quarters to the library. Complicating matters were that Abe and Hellboy were not in peak condition although Hellboy could feel the adrenaline flush away the buzz, like so many hopes and dreams.

Abe seemed to be rallying, too, and insisted they check the library—his telepathic touch made that a priority. Hellboy was fine with that since it was a room that brought comfort and assuring it was safe sounded swell. When they arrived, though, the massive doors were ajar and that spelled trouble. Without weapons, they rushed through the doors and sure enough, Nuada and Nuala were both there, the princess with her back to them. The handsome, cold prince looked over her shoulder at them and he scowled.

Wisely, they hung back by the doors to assess the situation. Agents and Manning, still in his suit, arrived in numbers, not that they could stop the mad prince. In the foreground stood

Abe, in his black garb, Hellboy shirtless but still wearing his overcoat, the Samaritan at the ready, and Liz, in a simple black T-shirt and dark pants, hands on her hips, ready to dish out some pain—she so felt like sharing pain right about now.

"Princess!" Abe called as he saw her. At the cry, Nuada spun his sister around so she could face them and the look of terror on her face made them freeze. Hellboy could only imagine what Abe was feeling right about now.

"No, Abraham, don't!" she called out. "He'll kill you!"

That brought a distasteful look to the prince's face and he asked, "Abraham?"

The intimacy seemed to infuriate him, resulting in the sudden appearance of his sword, the sharp tip now against her throat. Hellboy saw her swallow reflexively. The fireplace threw off a glow that reflected off the blade and cast bright spots around the room. Even though he was more alert than he had been five minutes ago, he could not trust himself to try to prevent twin from harming twin.

Abe remained a statue and Hellboy felt for him.

"Yes," the prince sneered with contempt. "I'll kill you too, Abraham, every one of you—if that's necessary."

To prove his intent, he allowed the sword to pierce her skin, just enough to cause blood to well up around the tip.

What astonished the agents, though, was that a matching cut appeared on the prince's cheek and red blood pooled and then ran down his own cheek. He didn't wince at the pain.

Calculating quickly, Hellboy knew that seeing Nuala in pain would cause Abe to act and probably act rashly. He was not trained for this sort of thing but Hellboy was. Without Krauss or Manning to give orders, he was going to have to take charge of the situation. He needed to save the princess, apprehend the prince, and save the world. That it might happen in this sanctum gave him the courage to try.

He stepped forward, away from the doorway, and neared the prince, who watched without doing further damage with the dagger. Nuala's eyes silently pleaded with him to hold his ground. Once more, he was going to have to disappoint a woman.

"Great," he said as he moved. "Then, why don't you just start with me, your Royal Assness?"

Nuada looked at Hellboy as if for the first time. After all, he'd already survived Wink's attack at the market and then, just hours before, handled the elemental. He could no longer be casually dismissed, no matter how arrogant the prince was. Nuada had no way of knowing how injured or tired or strong Hellboy was and to be honest, Hellboy wasn't entirely sure how much gas he had left in the tank. This was going to be as much bluff as anything else. Still, he held an advantage over the pretender to the throne. As a result of the mental calculations, the prince lowered the sword and, with his free hand, actually pushed his sister to the ground. She collapsed without protest, which was probably for the best.

Walking to meet his opponent halfway, Nuada instructed his sister, "If you move—I'll kill your Abraham first."

With another step, he smoothly extended the sword. He held it out like an extension of his right arm and to Hellboy's surprise, it extended further. The thing was very thin, especially the blade, but on both sides of the blade were intricate designs in greens and golds. A rounded and vertical rectangular space was toward the base which appeared attached to a sturdy metallic shaft with delicate filigreed designs all the way down. It was a sword turned lance and gave him an advantage.

"And your weapon?" he inquired.

Hellboy grinned and held up his massive stone right hand and replied, "Five-fingered Mary."

Nuada nodded as if to approve of the choice, like he had an option, and moved the spear, now parallel to the ground, its tip aimed at Hellboy's chest. At that motion, the shaft's base flared open revealing fletchings to guide it through the air. As they neared one another, first Manning then Krauss rushed through the doorway and skidded to a halt beside Abe, who remained fixed in place.

The prince waited for Hellboy to make the first move and Red obliged, feinting left then moving right and whipped around. The prince leapt high and jabbed the rushing Hellboy with the spear, slicing open his coat.

"Will you hand me the piece?" he asked Nuala over his shoulder.

His twin, still on the ground, shook her head no. Good girl, Hellboy thought.

The combatants circled one another, moving around the length and breadth of the sizable library. A fist swung through empty air matched by a thrust from the spear, usually missing its mark. As they neared the B.P.R.D. agents, they wisely scattered out of the way, none daring to interfere for fear of distracting their champion. The room was utterly silent save their footsteps and breathing. Even the fireplaces seemed to crackle at a lower volume.

Each time they neared one another, the nimble prince struck out, his reach far superior given the advantage of hefting the spear. He also was a quick athlete, who ducked, dodged and avoided each thrown punch, at first angering then enraging Hellboy. While the fists missed, the spear did not, slicing through Hellboy's clothes and ripping into his skin. Each pierce brought a fresh trickle of blood, greeted with a grunt, but that was all. He never landed a single blow. That began to worry him, until one time he timed Nuada's move perfectly and as the prince bent low to avoid the stone fist, he opened himself up to a low left jab. The prince was stunned, tottering in place.

"H.B., no! Stop—you mustn't harm him!"

Hellboy, momentarily distracted, looked across at Abe. "What do you want me to do?"

Before Abe could reply, there was a whistling sound in the air followed by a wet, ugly sound. Suddenly the spear tip was imbedded in Hellboy's chest, fresh blood oozing out and staining his coat.

"You may have mused in the past, 'Am I mortal?' " Nuada casually said, keeping his distance but clearly strutting like the victor.

Hellboy sneered at him, trying to avoid appearing hurt. Holding his ground, his right arm came up and he gave the spear a savage yank but the metal shaft broke, leaving the blade still inside his chest. Breathing was becoming a real challenge and he heard himself wheeze.

"Well, you are now."

Mortal didn't feel very good and he was having trouble getting a good breath. His eyes rolled upward and only Krauss's quick moves caught his heavy body before it crashed to the floor.

Nuada walked to the far side of the library and once more took possession of his sister, helping her to her feet. Then he looked around the room, seeking out Abe. Once he had found the amphibian, who was kneeling by his comrade's side, the prince addressed only him.

"Many people died for that crown." He gestured to the prone Hellboy, then added, "Many more will." It sounded like a fact, delivered without heat.

To everyone's surprise, Hellboy half rose, then reached his full height. Nuada actually blinked in surprise and his body language shifted, readying to defend himself anew. Hellboy moved his fists in the air, pantomiming that he was ready to resume their fight. Instead, the prince collected his sister in his powerful arms.

"If you want to save him and see her again, you'll bring me the missing piece," he told Abe with a note of finality.

Nuada, surprisingly, took a step back as Hellboy advanced. After a step or two, though, the hulking, wounded agent faltered. Abe reached out to support his friend but Hellboy utterly collapsed to his knees.

Liz shrieked, "Red—Red—no . . ."

A rush of agents filled Hellboy's field of vision, guns drawn, ready to keep the prince from inflicting further harm. His vision was getting hazy, but one thing he knew—at the far end of the room, the prince and princess had vanished.

No more than five minutes after the agents had stormed the library, they hoisted Hellboy on their shoulders, and with careful steps moved out, carrying him to the medical bay, and all Liz could think of was it appeared to be a funeral procession with the agents as pallbearers. Her lover's shallow breathing was all that proved he remained alive. Her own breath caught in her throat.

Manning was shouting something into his cell phone and Krauss had lingered behind to secure the library. She and Abe accompanied the agents and he seemed lost. Liz could understand that.

Should Red die, she too would be lost.

Finally at the bay, they carefully placed him on the sole operating table and backed away, none saying a word or even meeting Liz's eyes. They had already written him off and were fearing for their loved ones and themselves. Perfectly natural, she knew, but she also hated them for it.

Abe was already turning various devices on, attaching leads all over Hellboy's chest and head, and then letting them take readings. As the monitors did their part, Abe extended his webbed hands over Hellboy's chest, sensing for something—she didn't know what. Her eyes rarely moved from the gooey, sticky piece of metal sticking out of her mate's sternum.

Withdrawing his hand, Abe quickly put on a surgical gown and then specially designed rubber gloves and goggles, keeping him sterile. He checked the monitors and saw how dangerously low they were.

Hellboy periodically opened his eyes and groaned weakly. He was dying and Liz felt that she should be dying with him, as linked to him as the royal twins were to each other.

Abe ignored the latest groan and studied a CAT scan monitor that showed a detailed rendering of Hellboy's organs—heart, lungs, arteries, and a few Liz could not identify. The images were sharper than the ones he had seen using the Schufftein goggles two nights previous, and lacked the half-consumed Cheetos. In the center was the spear head which moved, as if alive, and each minor change in position caused Hellboy to let out a cry of pain.

She'd had enough of studying—it was time for action.

"Abe, pull the friggin' thing out, why don't you?"

"I cannot. See?" He gestured at the monitor and the shifting foreign object.

"Every time I touch it—every time I come close to it—it moves closer to his heart. I don't know what else to do."

They looked silently at one another, the gravity of the situation painfully clear.

He then stated the obvious, but it needed saying. "The wound will not heal until the spear is removed . . . We're running out of time."

Liz was going to fight for her man, even if she had to do it by herself. He was not going to die because she had done nothing. Everything else could wait, even telling him about the baby.

"Then we go after the prince," she declared. "Get him to do it—but we have to find him first."

The silence stretched on as both considered exactly how to track someone so elusive and how to obtain the power necessary to get the solution out of him. She was beginning to see each option as a failure, one outcome bleaker than the previous one. Her thoughts were interrupted when Hellboy coughed and then began to speak, although he sounded very different. She'd never heard him this hurt, this close to death.

"Liz, you were asking . . ."

She leaned close, kissed his forehead, and said in a soothing tone, "Shh, don't talk."

"No, no—let me tell you: I know—what's important," he continued, ignoring her as always. This time she didn't mind. This was important to him and they might not get too many more chances for this conversation.

"It's you.

"I can turn my back on the world. All of it—so long as you stay with me."

She fought back the tears she felt coming, blinking them away and staying close to him. Liz promised, "I'll stay with you."

Her hand wiped sweat from his brow and he smiled at the touch.

"You are the best man I've ever met," she added and meant every word.

As Hellboy's head fell back to the pillow, he repeated, "Man . . ."

A somber gathering stood in the remains of the library as forensic agents completed their work, gleaning whatever they could about the prince and his capabilities. The fireplaces had gone out and no one bothered to relight them. None had eaten or slept since the attack some twelve hours earlier.

Abe was agitated that his best friend was lying near death and a woman he had quickly come to care about was missing, in danger from her brother, no less. Manning was fielding calls from Washington and fending off the media with varying degrees of success while Krauss seemed the most dispassionate. He ordered the agents about, no doubt following the B.P.R.D. manual on how to handle incursions into their home.

Liz was out of her mind with worry and craved action but knew better than to charge out into the wide world without knowing in which direction to start. Time was too precious to waste and she also did not desire to leave Hellboy, not now, not when there was a chance they would find a solution too late. Or not at all.

It was Krauss who noticed that they could retrieve the image burned into the desk and he concentrated the agents on that. A printout of the image was made into a negative and they were able to study it.

While Krauss examined it, trying to decipher the glyphs, Abe walked over to the bookcase that Nuada had turned upside down. He lifted up the volume of Tennyson that now carried more emotional weight for him beyond its beautiful words. Casually flipping pages, he stopped and turned one final page and revealed the final piece of the crown, the one the princess had hidden from her brother.

Seeing that brought Liz some measure of hope. She also watched as Abe surreptitiously hid it within his belt, a trump card for later use. The fewer who knew the piece's whereabouts, the better.

Krauss ordered the team to the conference room where they could finally make a plan of action. Liz was the first one out the door.

Once she, Krauss, Manning, and six regular agents were seated around the highly polished wood table, they set to work. Krauss held up the print, already scanned and now available on the monitors of the imbedded touch-screen computer interfaces at each seat.

"The cylinder pattern yielded coordinates," he announced. "Leading to County Antrim, Northern Ireland. The Giant's Causeway."

Abe quietly entered the room after checking on Red's vitals, and Liz gathered there had been little change. They still had time.

Liz knew of Northern Ireland—not the specific locale, but that was not going to stop her. She could learn on the flight over the Atlantic. "So we know where he is—we should get going," she said, starting to rise.

A canvas-and-metal hand rose and stopped her in place. She looked at him as if he were crazy for just sitting there. In a sympathetic voice, he said, "Agent Sherman, he'll demand the gold piece."

"So? We give it to him."

Manning shot a worried look at Krauss and she was ready to ignore him, much as Hellboy would have had their roles been reversed. It sort of felt good.

"No," Krauss said, shaking her from her private thoughts. "If we locate it, we must make sure it never falls into his hands."

"Hold on, here—what are you saying?"

He didn't answer immediately, surely a first for him. Or Manning, who looked shaken and somber. This wasn't feeling right and the silence punctuated that. Finally, Krauss spoke up.

"Agent Sherman. The Golden Army must not awaken."

This time she didn't fight back the tears. The words were a hard slap and she was shaken badly by their callous tone.

"You're going to let him die—is that it?"

"The risk is too great. It cannot be weighed against any one life. Even his."

The tears flowed and Liz's anger grew, like the flames she commanded. Turning in her swivel chair to confront Manning, she demanded, "*What about you?* He saved your life."

Manning studied his shoeshine.

"I—love—him. I will not let him die." Her words were final. Her intentions had been announced and they'd have to confine her to prevent Liz from helping him.

The tension in the room seemed to grow thicker with each passing second and allies had suddenly become obstacles. Krauss didn't make things any better when he predictably added, "I don't make the rules, Agent Sherman. But I don't break them. Even if I don't like them."

"So—you don't like it, uh? But you just go obey. Red was right about you."

That finally seemed to provoke a response from Krauss, one not taken from the manual or even Emily Post. He stiffened in his seat and turned toward her. She wished he had eyes to read and not just limited body language.

"May I remind you that I am the leader of this team."

Liz rose from her seat, shooting a determined look at Manning, then directing her words to Krauss, who remained immobile. "Sir—there's no doubt about that. That's what you are, Doctor Krauss—but if you ever were human . . . I'm sorry to say that's long gone."

Without awaiting a response, she stormed out of the conference room, ready to take on Nuada and the entire damned Golden Army on her own.

As the door closed, Manning turned to Abe, who had remained silent during the unfortunate exchange, and asked, "Find anything?"

"No. Nothing, yet," he said, one hand tucked into his belt, fingering the golden prize and keeping quiet about it.

"Well, keep looking!" Manning insisted, back to full bluster mode now that Agent Sherman had left. He then addressed the nameless horde of section leaders and commanded, "All of you—we know it's here."

Switching to sycophant mode, Manning turned to face Krauss, who continued to sit and keep his own counsel. "We'll find it, Mr. Krauss. When Tom Manning gets on the case, things get done. Done—done. One hundred percent . . . I guarantee it."

What no one could see was that Krauss was also reaching into his belt—but unlike Abe's gold piece, his metallic-tipped hands were rubbing against the velvet pouch he had taken from his quarters.

Liz had cooled off moments after leaving the conference room. Manning and Krauss made her burn with fury but she was no fool. She could not possibly fly off to Ireland on her own, without a clue or weapon beyond her internal power. She needed help and hoped for at least one ally.

And there he was. Abe was the first to leave the conference room and instinctively turned toward her while Manning and the others exited and turned in the opposite direction.

"We'll get him out of here," she said to the amphibian. "Go to Antrim. Find the Prince. You and I."

Abe seemed less resolute than she did and that gave her pause. Seeking confirmation, she leaned in close and studied his goggled eyes.

"Are you in?"

"There's no other way, is there?" He knew the answer but had to ask it aloud, hear the words from himself and from Liz. She shook her head, sealing the deal. The logistics would have to work themselves out on the fly, but they were used to that. Of course, the stakes were rarely this high, but she had no choice, and neither did he. Not if they intended to save the ones they loved.

"Then, let's go," he said.

CHAPTER EIGHTEEN

It wasn't often that they needed the Bureau's private jet, but Liz took comfort in the knowledge it was there, ready and fueled at all times. The jet was nondescript, like all B.P.R.D. vehicles, but it was far more attractive than the garbage truck. The interior was comfortably appointed for the passengers along with state-of-the-art communications gear and emergency medical supplies.

Liz's access badge got her into the hangar without a problem and she double-checked the medical supplies, more for her own peace of mind than anything else. She shoved thoughts about her pregnancy, about her relationship issues, and even her future into a deep, dark corner of her mind and closed the door. Right now she needed to be entirely focused on the here and now. He needed her and she was going to stand by his side come what may.

After all, she had decided, if the world was going to end during this war, she wanted to be beside Hellboy.

Abe followed her and went right to the cockpit where he began the preflight checklist routine. He was a pilot among his many skills, although it was one he rarely used and few knew about. After all, what would an amphibian know about flying? It was a joke he liked to use every now and then.

Of course, he had something to fight for, too.

She heard the engines start and Liz looked out the open hatch and spotted Hellboy ready to join them. He was moving awkwardly, each step making him wince, but the look of determination on his face indicated he was going to make it to Ireland and give himself every chance to beat this unseemly death. He glanced toward the doorway and she smiled at him, offering not only encouragement but her love. Inwardly, she shuddered seeing him suffer as he made his way up the metal staircase, but she refused to show him any pity. Instead, she took his hand and helped him come aboard.

"Coffee, tea, or me," she teased and received a tired but pleased grin from her beloved.

"Going anywhere?"

All eyes turned to a different doorway and there, framed for all to see, was Johann Krauss. He was in a newly refurbished containment suit and his voice resounded with its usual stuffiness. Once he had Liz and Hellboy's attention, he entered the hangar and approached the aircraft so he could be heard over the warming engines.

"Good evening, *meine Freunde.* Do you have an authorization to take that plane?"

She patted herself, as if looking for her boarding pass, but then Liz withdrew her B.P.R.D.-issued pistol and leveled it right at her superior. While she had been trained with a gun, she never shot one, usually relying on her innate pyrotechnics to get the job done. If she had to, though, she would fire—but then wondered how that would affect a gaseous body.

All pretense of politeness and respect vanished as she leveled her aim and said, "Don't try to stop us, Johann."

Hellboy gaped at her, proud of his girl and always happy to see Krauss suffer. The commotion attracted Abe's telepathic attention and brought him from the cockpit. He stood behind Liz, protecting Hellboy, showing a united front. The trio stood firm and Liz was proud of them.

"On the contrary," Krauss said. "I've been giving it some thought, and we should be able to save Hellboy."

He took several steps forward and Liz trained her gun on him but wasn't ready to pull the trigger. She would hear him out and then shoot, if necessary. To her surprise, he gestured toward Abe and addressed his next comments his way. "You see? Before my present condition took hold, I too, suffered a loss—and it was indeed the sources of my misfortune. You will learn about it one day."

As Krauss reached into his belt pocket, Liz was uncertain if he was going to withdraw some odd weapon and she tensed, her finger threatening to spasm and yank the trigger. It took her will to control her impulses. She then exhaled as she saw that he had withdrawn a velvet pouch. Krauss then tossed it across the distance to Abe, who snatched it in one hand. He reached inside to see a Victorian ring and he examined it, looking questioningly at Krauss. Liz saw the ring and suddenly realized there was a lot more to Krauss than she had imagined. There might even be a heart-shaped bit of gas in that suit.

"But for now, the tactical advantage is ours. Consider this: the prince lacks the gold crown. And without it, his army poses no threat. None at all."

Abe silently stared at Krauss.

"We have permission to take off, then?" Liz asked.

Krauss drew closer to the plane and looked right at Liz. As he approached, she heard Hellboy groan out loud and her focus shifted from the ring and Krauss's heart to the piece of metal inching toward Hellboy's heart. They had to get airborne and fast.

"Agent Sherman . . . Liz . . . screw the rules," Krauss answered. He began to climb the stairs to join them and as he passed her in the doorway, he added, "Sometimes to know the beat—you've gotta be on the beat."

The kitchen had been long closed and all Manning wanted was a cup of coffee. His only choice was the vending machine down the hall from the conference room. Bright lights from the outdoor perimeter shone through the windows, decorating the hallway with splashes of yellows and whites. A few agents accompanied him, giving him an audience for his running commentary on the sorry state of the world.

His agency had been exposed for all the world to see, his biggest asset (and biggest pain in the asset) was mortally wounded, and the entire world was being threatened by a prince with an ages-old mad on. Whatever hopes he had for coming up with a brilliant bit of damage control would be dramatically helped if he could get a fresh infusion of caffeine.

So of course, the machine ate his coins and refused to dispense said caffeine.

Clenching his fist, he rapped it once, twice, against the front of the machine. The large illuminated image of a steaming cup of java mocked him as the lights winked at him and finally a cup emerged and settled in place. Then . . . no liquid inspiration.

The four agents watched him, keeping silent vigil, flanking him between the machine and the window. None offered a suggestion or tried to aid him.

"Latte—I command you—latte."

The coffee machine refused to accept the verbal command. He stared at it, thinking that the whole world was conspiring against him. The four agents remained at attention. "Why . . . why is this not working? I want this *fixed!*"

He glared at the four men, snapped his fingers, and they all withdrew pads from their coat pockets and jotted notes with funereal expressions.

"I want it working. Oh, jeez . . ."

His attention was finally diverted from the recalcitrant vending machine and he gaped at the nearest television monitor, tuned, as usual, to CNN. The usual cookie-cutter, well-coiffed woman, an Asian this time, looked at the camera. As a result, the machine chose that moment to finally begin boiling and serving coffee in the patiently waiting cup. Absently, looking at the screen, Manning reached for the coffee, scalding the back of his left hand. He bit his tongue to avoid making a pained sound.

The news reader continued, as an image of some oddly shaped building shifted to a picture of Manning, taken from the auction-house debacle, appeared behind her. She intoned, "The opening of the new facilities had its first setback when an air-conditioner unit failed to work properly, leaving dozens of celebrities sweating under the lights. Sign of things to come, or beginner's mistake? Mr. Symes wouldn't comment on it.

"In other news: Most of the explanations about the Blackwood Auction House incident in Manhattan have failed to persuade the experts and months of intense scrutiny lie ahead for the Bureau of Paranormal Research and Defense. Recent polls show that a majority of Americans favors a congressional investigation of the B.P.R.D. and its promotion of interspecies marriage, seen by many as a threat to traditional families, fueled by federal funds."

I'm a dead man, Manning thought. *My career is over. I have no future. I hate my life.*

He stared at the screen, unaware that his moment had passed and his face had faded, to be replaced by a picture of a wedge of Swiss cheese. "On the health front: A panel of experts in Switzerland has declared that prostate inflammation is to be blamed in excessive cheese consumption. Long, unruly hair and a receding hairline are also to be blamed, they say . . ."

"Damn it—damn it . . ." Manning muttered as he placed the cup back into the machine and let it fill with the last of the latte. The scalded hand went up to his mouth and he sucked it for comfort.

"How on earth can they blame me for cheese," he asked and stopped as the anchor finished her report.

"Both Dr. Johann Krauss and Dr. Thomas Manning will be called to testify . . ."

"Oh, jeez. Can't get any worse than this."

He heard the machine finally finish its work and he looked, seeing that his carelessness had left him with barely one-third of a cup. Okay, that's just par for the day.

Blowing into the cup to cool the remaining drink, ready to savor it at last, he heard a rumble. It was a familiar sound and was growing in volume. He then noticed that the latte was vibrating in his cup.

A shadow fell over the window, and Manning dreaded looking at its cause. Sure enough, the B.P.R.D. jet flew nearby, gaining altitude by the second. He knew in his heart who was aboard. As it roared by, he spilled more of the coffee, watching some splatter on his suit pants and shoes.

"Oh, dear . . . um, was that—our plane?"

Antrim, Northern Ireland
9:00 A.M.

Normally, a flight across the Atlantic would have delighted Liz, who never went anywhere. The notion of visiting Ireland or England or Switzerland would have been thrilling and she had more than once indulged in daydreaming about vacationing in one of those locales with Hellboy. Abe told her to get rest, not just given the last few days, but also out of concern for her health and the health of the baby growing by the day within her. Although she desperately wanted to tell him about it, she didn't dare bring up something so shocking when he was hurting this much.

He had to live to meet his son. Or daughter.

He had to live for her.

Rather than sleep, she gave up and decided to study. No doubt Abe knew everything they needed to know about the mystical secrets of the land; all she knew about was leprechauns. She instead read up on the terrain since the Giant's Causeway consisted of some forty thousand basalt columns that interlocked.

There was more she needed to understand and decided, now that Krauss had taken the stick out from his butt, maybe he'd be helpful. He had largely kept to himself for the first leg of the flight, for which she had been grateful.

She switched seats to one next to him and he put down his book as she approached.

"May I help you, Agent Sherman?"

"I like it better when you call me Liz," she said with a smile.

"Liz, then."

"Yes, you can, Dr. Krauss."

"Johann, please."

She smiled and nodded. "What happens if the Golden Army is activated?"

"If the legends are accurate, and Princess Nuala made it seem the texts were that, the Golden Army is an unstoppable force," Krauss said. "Nearly five thousand magically powered mechanical beings that followed direction without question. They need neither food nor rest. Once they were set upon mankind, they would not stop until our race ceased to exist."

"Five thousand marching soldiers could eradicate six billion people?"

"I know it sounds impossible, Liz, but it's true. They would likely be supported by the combined forces from the Children of the Earth and they too would overwhelm our armed forces. On a percentage basis, the number of armed combatants worldwide would pale in comparison with their brute strength."

Liz grew quiet, processing the lesson and recognizing the long odds. "There's no keeping them, then?"

"The soldiers? No. Control the crown, then you can stop them. Of course, as we have seen, Prince Nuada is not easily subdued. If he assembles the crown, then wresting it from his brow would prove most daunting."

"Do you have a plan for keeping him from reaching his goal?"

"Liz, right now we need to save Hellboy. Since the prince lacks the final third of the crown, we have some time. Once he's healthy, we can determine the best course of action."

She gave him her best smile, pleased that their priorities were finally in sync.

They were descending to the northeast coast and it looked well preserved, looking much as it had for the last millennium or two, with the column tops forming stepping stones, the tallest measuring some thirty-six feet high. Thanks to it being a National Nature Reserve in addition to being named a World Heritage Site, the entire area was pristine, green, and lush, and was the island's most popular tourist spot.

If only the UN knew what they were really preserving, she thought.

As they flew, and she fretted over her unborn child, Abe no doubt pulled strings and arranged for them to land on a stretch far from the public spot. Standing in the doorway as the ladder unfolded into position, Liz admired the greenery, deeply inhaled the fresh air (or fresher than New Jersey's air for starters). It was pretty and peaceful and the notion that deep below slept an army that was poised to ruin the planet for eons was unfathomable.

Hellboy was by her shoulder and carefully she snaked an arm around his waist, wordlessly lending him support. Together, they eased down the stairs and paused on the ground. As Abe and Krauss followed, sealing up the plane, the couple slowly worked their way to a hill that had been worn smooth by the countless seasons. She marveled at the basalt columns, dark, tall, and very imposing. The air was silent, not even a breeze to rustle the well-trimmed grass.

When Hellboy needed to rest, Krauss used the break to open up an old hand-colored map and pointed out their destination, a large ornately inscribed door.

"It should be here, someplace. The entrance should be here," Abe insisted as he looked one way, then the other.

"I bid you welcome, strangers. May I be of assistance?"

Four heads looked one way, then the other. Finally, Hellboy looked up and found a large, jet-black raven perched atop one of the taller columns. It sat there watching them with wise, old eyes. Liz knew it was no ordinary raven—nothing was as it seemed anymore.

"Thank you, uh, Mr. Raven. We would be grateful," she said to it, making certain her voice betrayed no panic or mockery.

Next, coming from between two of the basalt towers, was a legless goblin, moving along on a rickety wooden cart with a single wheel which was strapped to its stumpy waist. The goblin's sunken chest boasted medals from long-forgotten wars and other assorted trinkets that were all he had to mark his long life. He wheeled himself closer to the quartet, eyed them suspiciously and asked, "What are you looking for?"

Liz looked from the speechless raven to the unattractive goblin and told him, "We seek safe passage to Bethmoora."

The naming of the ancient revered land made both goblin and raven react, but they were subtle and remained silent for a long moment and she began to despair.

Wheeling closer to Liz, the goblin looked at her with hungry eyes, rubbing a grimy hand across his chin. "And what would a nice little girl like you want in the night lands . . ."

She opened her mouth to answer but she sensed a presence behind her, but it wasn't Red. Looking over her shoulder she was surprised to see canvas and metal. Krauss leaned in close and quietly said, "Careful, Liz."

Not Agent Sherman. Liz. That was going to take getting used to but she could adjust. What's one more adjustment given everything else going on in her life?

"We are looking for Prince Nuada," she said to the nameless goblin.

"Him I know."

The raven flew to the cart, interested in the conversation. The goblin acknowledged the bird as if it were an old friend.

Krauss stepped between Liz and the odd pair, seemingly protecting her, and she seemed okay with that now. "What will it cost?"

"Trade me something," the goblin said in an avaricious voice.

With a gesture, Krauss called the others together and they huddled, their backs to the curious onlookers. Liz listened to the ideas going back and forth as they tried to figure out what might appeal to a goblin—or a raven—that would be sufficient to gain access to Bethmoora. There was also the need to retain their weaponry, although Liz had the edge, given her weapon was herself. Finally, they settled on several options and broke formation. She half expected Krauss to have them cheer and slap hands like a football team. Thankfully, he still had his stuffiness.

He walked over to the goblin who eagerly eyed him.

Krauss gestured to his waist and said, "I have a . . . shiny belt."

Sadly, the goblin shook his head slowly, from one side to the other. He pointed to his absent legs and replied, "But I have no pants."

Liz realized they should have prioritized the options, especially since the raven had no use for the belt either. She chose to take charge with the negotiating, certain she could do better than an ages-old gasbag.

"Here," she said, taking off her binoculars and holding them up by the strap. "A wonderful set of magic eyes that will bring the world . . ."

The goblin cut her off in an annoyed tone, tiring of their feeble efforts. "I already have binoculars! But I see something special . . ." And his voice faded away, letting his leering look finish the sentence.

He was directing his attention to Hellboy, who was hunched over, struggling to stay on his feet unaided.

Liz couldn't imagine what the goblin would want with him. She needed him and that was non-negotiable. Even Krauss wouldn't bargain away a living being.

The goblin pointed at Red's chest, the finger bobbing up and down. "Under his bandage. Something shiny. Something nice."

The others gaped at Hellboy's chest, knowing the spear tip resided there, moving with every heartbeat. Then they looked back at the goblin, who crossed his arms like a child, ready to settle for nothing less.

"I want that, in exchange for your crossing!"

She shook her head and bent low, filling the goblin's field of vision. Once Liz was certain she had his undivided attention, she told him in a clear, steady, take-no-prisoners voice, "You can't take it out—not without killing him."

Nodding sagely, the goblin stroked his chin again, seeking a solution. The raven remained a silent witness.

Clouds began to fill the sky, a chill entering the air.

Finally, he stirred and a happy look crossed his careworn face.

"Mmm . . . maybe I know someone who can . . . Will you give it to me then?"

Without waiting for consensus, Liz nodded her head in agreement.

"Very well, then!" the goblin exclaimed, clapping his hands. The raven flapped its wings once to agree.

Tugging on one of the trinkets, it pulled out a chain and at its end was an engraved whistle, covered with grime, dented on one side. He took a few deep breaths to get ready then blew long and loud, the shrill sound making the bargainers wince.

Behind the goblin, several of the gray columns began to move, shaking the ground, making the others struggle to maintain their balance. Krauss lent support to Hellboy and Liz was grateful. But it was brief as she concentrated on watching stone come to life.

Rocks, dirt, plant life were shaken free as a second arm emerged. When the second arm was freed, they craned their necks to see the fully assembled, stone life form—at least from the waist up. It sat still, erect and waiting under the cloud-filled sky.

Liz noticed its chest. Inscribed on it were familiar markings and she realized they matched the symbols on the map. Below it, the stomach contained the doorway they sought.

A second, shorter whistle sounded and the door opened. They could glimpse through it a darkly lit land.

Bethmoora.

A third whistle and the doorway closed with a dull sound.

The goblin looked at the quartet and said, "Once you pay—you get out."

CHAPTER NINETEEN

The bargain sealed, the stone gateway opened again and this time the legless goblin led the B.P.R.D. agents through the dark, stone archway and into the legendary land of Bethmoora. The "legendary land" struck Liz as monochromatic, bleak, and forbidding. The vibe she picked up from the place was not a good one as the hairs on the back of her neck rose to attention. It was quiet, like a very large mausoleum, and the air was stale, in need of freshening from the outside world. Too long, she imagined, Bethmoora had sealed itself off from the land above. Had there been more contact between the Children of Man and the Children of the Earth, she wondered, would Nuada still be so hellbent on destroying one to preserve the other? As Krauss explained during the flight, the truce between man and elf had essentially sealed off all contact between the worlds for thousands upon thousands of years. Only now, with Nuada seeking to stir up a new war, was Bethmoora entertaining humans for the first time in even goblin memory.

The obsidian stonework continued well past the archway and the new land. Liz studied the formations, fascinated at first and then horrified to discover that goblins had been burned to a crisp and had actually become one with the stone structures. Whatever crimes were committed, the punishment was most certainly harsh and without hope of reprieve.

The walk down the hill and into the land of fable was slow as the group took turns supporting Hellboy as they followed behind the goblin, who effortlessly pushed himself along. The slope and gravity, still a constant even in this fantasy land, no doubt had much to do with his ease of movement. At least they were making progress and she only hoped that it was happening with time to still save his life and then prevent a holy war that would scorch the earth clean.

"You should've seen this city when it was alive," the goblin, who continued to refuse to identify himself, said as they cleared the archway.

Abe, who was nearest to him, asked, "What happened to it?"

That caused the goblin to pause and as much as Liz wanted to hear the answer, fascinated as she had quickly become with the place, now was not the time for a new history lesson. Still, she stopped, her right shoulder holding up Hellboy, digging into his armpit and supporting the weight, the hand aimed upward and holding his own. Her free hand rested on her belly.

Gazing ahead, she saw the signs of civilization. In the gloom before them, there were silhouettes of twisted, dark hovels, visible in a valley below, thanks to the roaring fireplaces and candles near the windows.

The goblin gestured for them to continue, now that they knew they were near others and should be careful. After several minutes they reached the outskirts of the town, denoted by a cobblestone street that had missing stones. On either side were fallen or cracked columns. The first buildings on the street were tumbledown structures that could not possibly house anyone, goblin or man. Clearly, Bethmoora was not a happy place for its inhabitants. She wondered how many were left and would any join in Nuada's cause?

"A curse," the goblin finally said in answer to Abe's query. "As soon as the Golden Army was stored in here . . . a plague of silence and darkness befell us. And the world left us behind.

"For a long time only I dwelled in the dust."

He continued forward until they reached a squat, dark dome, half-buried in sand. It was obvious that the land was barren, unable to support vegetation for food, and there was a lack of cooking smells in the air. Not a good sign. Nor was the absence of insect or bird life. Even the raven remained outside with the stone giant.

"But many winters ago, one of the seven Angels of Death came to rest. And she never left."

Liz and the others started at the mention of an Angel of Death, let alone that there were seven in existence. She knew about life and death, and the deaths she had caused in her wake. Killing tooth fairies was fine, killing others because she was young and out of control, not so fine. Those faces and those sounds haunted her to this day. Were the six other angels following her, collecting souls she had freed before their time? Liz Sherman had never before imagined an embodiment of death. Sure, there was the image of the Grim Reaper from Dickens or the pert young thing from the graphic novels or the happy-go-lucky fella from fiction she read as a teen, but not once had she imagined there were true harbingers of death.

Given all she had seen since encountering Professor Broom, she should not have been surprised, but was nevertheless.

Lost in thought, she nearly missed the goblin's next words, delivered in a whisper born of fear.

"She likes the quiet and the dark."

Authoritatively, he jabbed his hand toward the amphibian and their team leader.

"You two wait out here," he ordered, grabbing at Liz's hand.

"We will go inside."

With that, the goblin pushed himself forward as Liz urged her body to be strong enough to get Hellboy through this. He moved along, somewhat out of it, and she found herself missing the irreverent commentary that he would have normally given at this point.

Instead, she was left with imagining this land and all that had befallen it. The dome was like the rest of the place, cracked, pitted, and monochromatically gray. Whatever writing had covered the exterior was indecipherable given how much was missing. Sand covered some of the dome's outside and even more was piled in miniature dunes within. The light from outside was all that provided interior illumination so she had trouble seeing and stubbed one foot against a fallen stone. She stumbled over a second and nearly dropped Hellboy, who merely groaned louder than before, earning her a stern look from the goblin.

They went deeper within and the light grew less and less useful. Liz finally saw the goblin slow by a doorway to another room, so she adjusted her gait and then saw up ahead that someone awaited them.

The interior of the domed room had three tiers of stone shelves, carved from the walls, and atop them, ringing the room, were squat candles, the only source of illumination.

In the center was a dark, ancient figure, robed in a deep blue cloak, and hunched over a complex fresco, running in a wide circle. Liz finally determined that it was some sort of story in pictures but she wasn't close enough to glean what they were.

Using a long wand, the figure moved strange pieces, playing against some unseen opponent.

The goblin stood just outside the door as if even he dared not disturb the game player. Still, he was there to bargain and finally spoke up.

"Hello, old friend. I have brought you visitors."

With that, he moved into the room, Liz following. Hellboy didn't change as they neared the figure, the one she presumed was the Angel of Death.

The Angel of Death. One of seven. And now they were going to bargain with it. All that was missing was Woody Allen and a tennis court. Unlike the Fellini-esque Death who wore all black robes and moved ponderously, this mysterious figure was tall, muscular, and possessed massive dark wings that unfurled from its back and split into two, giving the appearance of four distinct wings. The weathered and cracked crest that rose from the cheeks upward and flared around in a semicircle flattened the head's appearance. It had canals for ears, she presumed, but was taken by the lack of eyes and featureless top half of the head. She recalled the goblin had referred to the Angel as a she but it appeared too muscular and asexual for a gender.

"And I have a favor to ask of you."

At that, the wings extended outward and Liz gasped when she saw that running across the covert of each wing was a set of human-looking eyes. Over two dozen eyes were open and staring, unblinking, at the trio.

Rising from its position at the game board, the Angel of Death approached them with slow steps. Whatever it was, Liz decided, it was very old and had clearly seen happier days.

In a raspy voice, dried from disuse, the Angel answered the legless goblin. "I owe no favor to you, goblin. Leave."

Liz's heart dropped at such a response. Her burden seemed all the heavier.

"But—I've done so much for you," the goblin said, fighting to remain civil and with some shred of dignity. "Brought you so many souvenirs. And he . . . he has something shiny, something mine."

The eyes all swiveled about and focused solely on Hellboy. If it was possible to see all these eyes widen at once, they did in recognition.

"Anung Un Rama!"

Well, that was certainly an interesting development, Liz thought. Did the Angel know all living beings, like Santa Claus?

"You know that name?" she asked the Angel.

The Angel's eyes turned their intense gaze on her and answered, "And yours, Elizabeth Sherman. I have been waiting for you both many a winter moon . . . I am his death and no one else's . . . and I will meet him at each crossroad."

The Angel of Death had been waiting for her. None of its siblings. This one. Here in Bethmoora. Liz was uncertain what that portended. Was she fated to die during this attempt to save Hellboy?

No, it said it had been waiting for Red, too.

Then she finally caught a glimpse of an image on the floor. It was a drawing of Hellboy, his horns fully grown, crouched before a snake with unknown symbols on its head. Below, on Red's upturned left palm, was a skull, and there were flames.

She craned her neck and saw other images, all tracing her lover's life. His birth, life, and, she supposed, his final act, were all there, drawn who knew how long ago and the Angel was waiting for him . . . them.

Was this entire trip a folly?

The goblin continued to bargain, holding up his end of their agreement. She was curious to see how this would play out, although the feeling of gloom that had enveloped her since entering Bethmoora now leeched the warmth from her body and she couldn't help but shiver.

"Can you get me that—what is mine?"

"Can you save him?" Liz asked, stepping forward, shoving her irrational fear aside and telling it to behave. She needed to be brave for them both.

The Angel considered them both and then gestured with its left hand. Beneath the hand, on the worn, sandy ground, small gusts of wind appeared and rearranged the sand. Grains marched this way and that, furrows were formed and shifted in obeisance to such a powerful figure. She was surprised to see a sand bust of herself, with a resolution to rival a digital camera. Another image was forming, that of Hellboy, but this was larger, more detailed, and went below the shoulders to include the chest and Nuada's spear tip.

She shivered anew.

"In this crossroad—it is for you to decide that."

Great, it was speaking in riddles. Better than tongues, she supposed, but right now she needed clarity.

"It's all the same to me," the Angel told her, each word devoid of emotion. "My heart is filled with dust and sand. But you should know: it is his destiny to bring about the destruction of the earth."

Liz was jolted by the revelation. Okay, maybe that was too much clarity. Could he be healed only to participate in the coming war and help bring about the end of the world?

As if reading her thoughts, the Angel bowed close to her and offered, "Not now, not tomorrow—but soon enough."

If that were true, and who was she to argue with an Angel of Death, then there was a chance the coming war could be averted. If so, she would deal with whatever the Angel implied was to come afterward. The Angel mentioned crossroads and that meant there were options, choices to be made. This was but one such turning point. A bargain now would mean more time and with time came possibilities.

"Knowing that—you still want him to live?"

If they survived then there would always be a fighting chance. And there would be time for him to know his child.

"Please."

The Angel nodded once in agreement. It backed away from her and paused, considering her words, which seemed odd to Liz. "The time will come," it finally said to Liz as all its eyes turned once more to her. "And you—will suffer more than anyone."

Hands on hips, she said firmly, "I'll deal with it. Now save him."

"It is done."

Liz wasn't sure what she had expected. Everything she had been raised to believe about heaven and hell, about monsters and demons, proved wrong. Now she expected a light show to outdo anything ever produced by ILM, to out-Spielberg Spielberg, but instead there were no pyrotechnics. No lights bursting in air. It was silent for a moment. Then a groan rose from the sandy floor. A sound Liz had never heard before. Hellboy was the source of the sound. Now that was odd. She'd heard him grunt in pain from everything ranging from a paper cut to being thwacked by the elemental. This was true pain, life-and-death pain, and she felt her heart beating faster, almost in time with his cries of discomfort.

A new sound filled the musty room. It was a rough cackle, coming from the Angel, and it was most unpleasant.

She ignored the Angel and focused on Red. He grimaced and cried out some more as the red-stained, silver- and gore-covered spear point removed itself from his chest. The lance's sharp edges cut into his bones, his veins, his lungs and skin—

but it was finally removed, and the blade hung suspended in the air, dripping pieces of Hellboy to splatter into the sand.

The goblin wheeled himself over to it and scooped it up, ignoring the gritty, sticky, disgusting condition of the object.

"Shiny," he said in obvious denial of the reality in his hands.

Liz amended, "My precious." She then looked at Hellboy who was on the ground and unmoving. The spear was gone, his life was saved—what was he waiting for?

"I've done what I can—now give him a reason to live," the Angel told her and then, its work completed, slowly dissipated into the air, its countless eyes the last part of it to vanish.

What was she to do? Clap her hands if she believed in fairies? Red wasn't Tinkerbell. This wasn't Never-Never-Land. She wasn't sure yet what Bethmoora was, but it was darker and more sinister than J.M. Barrie's fantasy world. No, she had to focus on the writhing, sweating figure huddled at her feet. He needed a reason to live and it just so happened, he had provided her with that very reason not long ago.

She gently placed her left hand on her belly one more time as she kneeled beside her lover.

Her partner.

Her mate.

Leaning close to his ear, she said quietly, "You are going to be a father, Red."

Liz then gazed at him with a hopeful, happy smile. There, she had said it out loud and everything felt real. Everything felt fine. He would be a daddy and they would defeat Nuada. They may not live happily ever after, but then again, who did? They'd fight and cry and disappoint one another but she was absolutely certain now they'd do it together till death do them part.

The words seemed to have their desired effect as his eyes opened and fluttered a few times, yellow beacons in the dimness of the dome. He then smiled in acknowledgement of the words.

She smiled back, crying freely for the first time—tears of joy and relief. Each drop falling from her cheek to his, each teardrop making him smile again and again.

Liz wished their private moment could have been preserved but the growling voice of the goblin interrupted them.

"All this is very touching," he said, sounding anything but touched, "But . . . if you still want to meet Nuada . . . we have to go."

Liz, her back to the goblin, bobbed her head once in agreement and whispered in Hellboy's ear. "Time to wake up, Red. We have to save the world."

"Again," he said, a wry grin indicating he was already feeling much better.

A few moments later, he was on his feet and she examined the wound as he regained his balance and made certain he could function. She stared at the rips in his coat and chest, seeing his lifeblood stain everything. But the bleeding had stopped and he didn't wince when he stood. Carefully, she traced the edges of the wound and understood they would leave a scar, a daily reminder of how close to death he had finally come.

Then, like a newborn, he took one step, then another. He grinned at her and even gave her a dopey thumbs-up.

"Let's get the others," she told the goblin, who was already wheeling toward the doorway. Taking Red's hand, they walked away from the game board of his life, away from the dried bits of blood-caked sand that would forever be a souvenir of their time here.

When they emerged from the dome, Abe and Krauss had been pacing, no doubt anxious and concerned. She had lost total track of time, much like the denizens of this realm, but imagined they must have been sick with worry.

Abe broke into a broad grin when they emerged and he rushed to Hellboy's side, and hugged him without hesitation. Red returned the gesture with gusto, proving he was rapidly coming back to normal. Maybe not perfect, but his spirit had been restored.

Krauss formally bowed in Hellboy's direction and Liz smiled as he returned the gesture with a sloppy salute. They were a team and ready to deal with Nuada.

The goblin rolled forward, again refusing all help. As they walked, Liz sketched out for them the Angel and the healing but neglected to include anything about the Angel's prediction about what their joint fate was to be.

Might be.

Instead, Krauss went into a discourse on the imagery devoted to the Angel of Death beginning with the formation of organized religion and how each pantheon of mythological gods portrayed the being. They were all too happy to have Hellboy back so no one complained.

Except the goblin, who laughed at some of the more outlandish descriptions. That only encouraged Krauss, who continued his discourse well into the twentieth century.

At last, though, they had left the desiccated village behind and were on a beaten dirt road that was the only passage through a vast underground area. There was no sign of life, no sounds, or even any distinct odors to mark the place. All that was to be seen was a wide, well-worn, but intact stone bridge.

The goblin stopped and gestured to the other side. "Here we are—and here they are . . . all seventy times seventy soldiers."

He seemed lost in thought as he led them across the bridge, recalling those horrible days that had come back to haunt them.

"Sometimes I wish we had never created them . . ."

Again he was lost in memory. She felt for him, since it was the first time he seemed to display genuine emotion.

"Bim-bam! went the hammers," he said suddenly, more to himself than the others. "Fwosh! went the furnaces. And one of them fires took my legs away . . . but build them we did."

She was startled to realize that the goblin dated back that far, countless ages past, a living witness to the original horrors. A part of her was thankful he had paid a price for such monstrosities.

The odd quintet reached the base of a massive staircase and Krauss walked past the goblin, ready to descend.

"This is as far as I go," the goblin spoke up. Krauss hesitated and the others hung back.

"I—I'm not very good with stairs. But if you are here to stop the prince I wish you luck then. The army must not be awakened," he warned them, the tone conveying his distaste for the army's creation.

Liz leaned over and kissed him gently on the forehead. He may have built the army, but he also helped her save Hellboy, and bargained honorably. She did not wish him ill.

"Undo what we did," he begged her. "Undo it."

She nodded in agreement and Hellboy placed a reassuring hand on her shoulder. It felt so good to have him back.

The long walk put more barren, desolate rock on display as they walked up and up, reaching further into Bethmoora. On the one hand, it was a chance to see something entirely different and probably the closest Liz would ever get to seeing an alien planet. On the other, she wished there was an elevator so Hellboy could finish recovering.

Still, she had to smile as he began to banter a bit with Johann and Abe.

"What do you think we'll find?" he finally asked Abe.

"There are too many possibilities to even begin guessing," he said. He wasn't smiling, despite the lightened mood. No doubt, he was concerned about Nuala, and it was quite a legitimate concern.

"I say the toy soldiers are in the world's biggest toy box," Hellboy suggested.

That got a noncommittal sound from the amphibian.

"What about you, Johann?"

"Like Agent Sapien, I cannot begin to fathom how King Balor would have seen to it they were safely stored."

"Take a guess," cajoled Hellboy.

"Mathematically, we are looking at a thousand to . . ."

Liz interjected, not wanting to be left out. "It's going to be something big and scary."

Abe looked over his shoulder at her.

"I feel it," she insisted.

"The odds are . . ." Krauss continued.

"Screw the odds," Hellboy said. "I'll go there with the missus."

The missus. That sounded nice, she considered. They had to get through this, talk about the pregnancy, their future, and so much more.

"*Mein Gott.*"

Krauss's stunned words made them all peer up and gaze across the distance.

Unfortunately, Liz was right. They were staring out at a vast, ornately decorated holding area for the soldiers, all safely encased in giant, decorated golden eggs, each one nestled in an alcove carved into the sheer rock which extended upward for hundreds of feet. It was as if they were some silent audience in the largest coliseum ever conceived. Each row consisted of several dozen golden eggs and then the rows stretched up and back into the shadows, making a count impossible. The math she did in her head said there were nearly five thousand eggs in this space, a terrifying number given their size and reputation.

At the bottom, standing under a mammoth statue of a weeping soldier—Balor, perhaps?—as if he had been awaiting them all this time, was a single figure.

Nuada.

CHAPTER TWENTY

Even the prince seemed dwarfed by their surroundings. In his time, Hellboy had seen some impressive sights, but this one took the cake. Not only was this arena beggaring the imagination, but by its sheer size and scope, the place felt more like a temple. It spoke of ages gone by and happier times.

He, Liz, and the others stood at one end of a long and wide marble platform. At their end appeared to be turbines, easily twice his size, set into the stone flooring. Huge golden gears were set one atop the other, horizontally fitted to the slate-gray flooring. They were clean, polished, not showing any sign of age or disuse. That meant they were ready to work, something he sort of hoped would gum up the prince's plans. At the other end was the prince, looking none the worse for wear, his sword at his side. He gestured, playing to a silent audience of eggs, looking maybe a tad vulnerable now that Wink was no longer shadowing him.

"You brought the remaining piece, I presume," he said. No questions were being asked; it was stated as fact.

He was resplendent in a taupe robe with wide shoulder pads and red leggings ending in polished black boots. Nuada stepped aside and revealed, from some unknown place, his twin sister. That prompted a response, a gurgled noise from Abe.

Krauss moved forward, standing beside Hellboy, and replied, "No . . . we did not . . ."

Whatever he was about to say was stifled by a raised hand.

"I am not addressing you . . . talking bag."

The prince then looked past him.

"Abraham?"

Hellboy, Krauss, and Liz turned to focus on Abe, who held the final gold piece of the crescent crown in his webbed hands.

"Abe . . . you didn't . . ." Hellboy said in a disappointed voice.

Abe looked directly at his friend and said, "What would you do? If it were Liz?"

That seemed to explain everything and in his heart, Hellboy understood. There was much he had done in her name and much more he would be willing to do. He was happy Abe had finally found the one who could prompt such loyalty, but the circumstances sure sucked.

He nodded in understanding.

Crossing the distance, the others trailing slightly behind him, Abe approached the prince and then, keeping a safe space between them, delivered the final piece.

The prince fit the golden piece between the other two and Hellboy was intrigued by the way the pieces seemed to complete one another, forming a seamless crown that had not been whole for centuries.

Satisfied the crown was knit back together, with no proclamations or any clerics to witness the coronation, Nuada simply placed it on his head.

Just when Hellboy thought he was free from the usual pompousness, the prince proclaimed in a loud voice, "I am Prince Nuada, Silverlance, leader of the Golden Army. Is there anyone who disputes my right?"

His words echoed and died in the far recesses of the arena. No response was forthcoming from the silent eggs. His sister also stood, a mute witness to his proclamation.

King Nuada turned his attention to the four beings before him. Hellboy figured the four could take him, maybe five if the sister wanted a piece of the man for offing their dad. He tensed, ready to pounce, and felt that he was still healing, not at all at peak efficiency. That hadn't stopped him before and he would be damned if that would stop him now.

Of course, if the Angel were right, he was already damned— but that was a philosophical matter for some other time. He looked at the newly crowned king, whose expression seemed bored or dispassionate.

"Kill them."

They were simple words but ones that carried with them royal power. He said it softly enough for the quartet to hear, but once carried on the air, they had a magical effect on the thousands upon thousand of eggs.

There was a deep rumble under their feet and their ears were filled with the sounds of well-oiled mechanisms coming to life. He could tell there were gears, ratchets, and springs in use. Row after row of eggs came to life and were opening up, unfolding using elegant goblin technology. Like flowers blooming in a new spring, the eggs unfolded and spread apart, revealing the coiled, folded metallic forms of the Golden Army. Hellboy craned his head to note that they were entirely surrounded by the eggs, easily outnumbered and out-armed.

Studying their forms, he recognized that they were going to be larger than any of the agents. He looked up and saw that the now fully re-formed soldiers were huge. They were at least ten feet tall, and maybe twice as wide as the B.P.R.D. team was. Each had an oval, beaked head with black eyes, affixed atop a swivel that replaced the neck. Their bulbous shoulders gave way to thin arms that ended with three heavy, paneled forearms that encased the fingers. The soldiers were similarly designed for their legs, although there was a knee join and the shins were flat panels of gold. Around the joints and where the heart and lungs would be on a human were open spaces that pulsated with red light, indicating each member of the army was operational.

Each egg also seemed to contain a lance and shield that each soldier retrieved once it stood erect and glowing with resumed life. The weapons appeared to be made from the same metallic substance and no doubt would prove formidable.

Nuada was also watching, glorying in the rebirth of the legendary army now under his command. Nuala, though, was far less pleased and shrank away from her brother. He grabbed her roughly by the arm and led her back to the marble throne that awaited them, under the gargantuan statue.

Abe was aghast and turned to Hellboy saying, "He—he lied to us!"

The soldiers were still waking up, lining up in some pre-programmed formation so there were scant seconds left before they would engage them. Still, Hellboy took in his friend's anguish and leaned in to him with a weary grin. "Abe, old buddy. If we survive this, we need to talk."

Abe nodded sadly and Liz looked panicked.

Time to move. In unison, although with far less precision than their robotic opponents, they began to retreat back toward the staircase. Unfortunately, the arena was in the round so there were hundreds of soldiers at every turn.

The army broke into battalions or columns or whatever it was they did in smaller numbers and the nearest moved on them in lockstep. As a result, the access to the staircase, and freedom, was denied the team. Instead, they were being herded to a nearby wall and soon they were pressed up against the smooth marble that formed the lower barrier between floor and stadium.

A phalanx of golden soldiers approached, their right arms slashing through the air, threshing invisible wheat or readying to slice the B.P.R.D. agents into ribbons. The time to fight was upon them.

With a glance, Hellboy noted that Nuada had seated himself on the throne, the brazier nearby reflected off the golden crown encircling his head. Nuala was nearby—unable to leave, unable to help.

"The fire is in me," he heard Liz begin to chant. From her hands and around her body, blue flame sprang to life, ready to be unleashed. Her eyes looked determined but the sweat upon her brow showed how concerned she was. Liz wasn't a brawler, let alone a soldier. This wasn't a life she had asked for but it was one she was willing to share with Hellboy. They had absolutely no time to talk about her pregnancy so all he knew was that somehow, despite the odds, they had conceived new life. That had to be protected at all costs. He then wondered, with some degree of worry as the slashing blades came ever closer, if her fire could injure the baby. Nuts, she shouldn't be here. None of them should be.

Resigned to the inevitable, he reached to his side and retrieved his Samaritan, taking aim at the army coming at them. He shot Liz a look that told her to wait.

"No," he told her. "Let me. I wanna see if they're really mind readers . . ."

"Indestructible," Abe finished.

"That."

The Samaritan was unleashed and bullet after bullet hit their targets dead on. Weak he might be, but his aim remained strong. Still, each bullet reached a solider, dented the metal, and then stopped. None penetrated the armor and each bullet was pushed out, dropping to the floor as the metal repaired itself. Goblin magic.

He ran forward, toward the soldiers and then went into a slide, positioning himself directly beneath them. As he slid, he fired again.

Several did manage to pierce the metal casing this time, one going so far as to cause the internal wheelworks to explode. As the damage was done, it was undone.

They were invincible, indestructible, and unstoppable.

"Mmh," Hellboy grunted.

Holstering the Samaritan, he crouched low and then sprung into the air, his stone right arm rearing back and ready to deliver a mighty blow. He landed on a shoulder, grabbed onto the rim of a chest, and swung down in a straight arc. His stone hand did its job, smashing in the head, which sank out of sight, inside the pulsating red lights. Without waiting, he pushed off, only to land on another and smack that one too. The third received a crippling blow to its chest, causing springs and jagged-toothed wheels to explode outward in a shower of red sparks.

As he leapt for the fourth soldier, he noticed that unfortunately, his fists caused as much damage as his bullets. In other words, none whatsoever.

The three damaged robots resumed their pristine condition and continued to march toward the others.

New soldiers, though, reached to their side and ripped a section of stone column free. Each took a piece and battered Hellboy with it, knocking him to the ground. The blows caused him tremendous pain and when the column met marble floor, it left cracks and crevices.

One final soldier approached Hellboy, raised its section of stone column, and prepared to deliver a killing blow with mathematical precision.

At that moment, Johann Krauss was also being confronted by a single soldier. It loomed over him and spread its arms apart, ready to bring them together in a mighty blow that was sure to kill a normal mortal.

Krauss was anything but a normal mortal. He quickly accessed a valve on his chest, releasing his ectoplasmic form just as the two metallic arms swung closed.

The arms met, pressing the empty canvas suit flat, but Krauss was gone. In fact, the gaseous form seeped into the robot's body. The crimson light flickered once and then shifted to the blue end of the spectrum.

The robot turned to face Hellboy, who was being helped up to his knees by Liz. They stared at him with some confusion.

Now in control of the robot, Krauss wheeled it about and thrust its lance into a fellow soldier's chest. One well-aimed thrust was followed by another and another, as the surrounding soldiers were damaged. Bits of golden metal and internal components were littering the ground near them.

Krauss's robot ripped off an arm and tossed it through another approaching soldier. A head was ripped off and tossed aside.

Some of the fallen had their lights grow dim, sparking with leaking life. Foul-smelling lubricants spilled out, turning the surrounding area slick.

Hellboy and Liz moved away, no longer immediate targets. He was still moving slowly, clearly in pain.

Seemingly unstoppable, he waded through the phalanx and then imitated them by grabbing a different marble column and ripping it free. Using it like a baseball bat, Krauss's robot smashed one approaching robot to the right, the next to the left.

Liz's fireballs whizzed by him on either side as she tried to provide covering fire. With great whooshing sounds, they at least slowed down those machines nearest Hellboy, letting Krauss concentrate on the other nearby enemies.

The problem was, for each fallen soldier, another filled in. There were just too many of them for even one rogue robot to make any difference.

To protect his friends, Krauss raised the robot's fists, challenging all comers for a brawl. Three immediately accepted the challenge and stalked him until one broke from the back and launched itself at Krauss.

The others and more lined up to form a wall of crimson and gold. There was no escape.

The one that flew toward him extended sharpened lances, replacing its fists. It sliced into Krauss's chest and bits scattered.

Another charged Krauss but he managed to coax his robotic form to use the charging robot's momentum to lift up the enemy and toss it aside.

Worse, their programming recognized his robot as being counted as among the enemy. They surrounded him and their arms became sharpened blades. With ease, Krauss was quickly dismembered, stripped apart, his pieces scattered far enough so they could not reform. Like hyenas or jackals stripping a carcass clean, the controlled robot was no longer able to function.

One soldier approached Krauss and swung a bladelike arm right through the center of his chest, slicing him in two. Gravity took over and the twin pieces spread apart.

Krauss staggered and then his knees began to buckle. He looked up to see a wall of soldiers, and then, hurtling over them, one final soldier, its arms raised. As it arrived, the arms bent and the elbow sections crushed the robotic head deep within the chest cavity. Krauss's construct teetered, ready to fall, and the attacker continue to rip into it.

The head was ripped from the body and tossed aside, landing with a dull thud at Hellboy's feet. For once, he felt sympathy for Krauss and wondered if the gaseous life form could possibly have survived. Liz placed a soothing hand on his shoulder, silent in her own shock.

The head stopped glowing blue and went black, making them both think he must not have been able to survive such damage.

The head then blinked once, back in its original red. From beneath, spiderlike legs emerged, raising the head off the ground. It scuttled back toward its damaged body, which was finally being healed, slowly though, thanks to the goblin engineers. As it neared the body, a hand reached down and grabbed the head, replacing it in its original position, the feet helped form connections and voilà, it was good as new.

All that rage, all that destruction—for nothing.

They were dead.

Hellboy and Liz shared a long look that said the same thing and they were uncertain what to do. The army formed up once more, directly looking their way.

In the distance, they saw Abe duck, leap, bend himself in impossible contortions, but always manage to avoid a direct hit. He couldn't hurt them, but at least he was avoiding being hurt himself.

"I'm out of ideas."

Startled, Hellboy looked over his right shoulder and there was Krauss, once more in the containment suit, sounding defeated.

But alive. That gave Hellboy hope. And a notion.

"I have one," he said.

Weak from the loss of blood, Hellboy hauled himself to his feet. He shook himself, making certain everything worked. Liz and Krauss gaped at him as he turned his back to them and looked across the arena to where Nuada still sat. All he needed was a foam hand with a raised index finger.

"Hey you—Prince Namajama—I challenge your right to command this army!"

No sooner did the words end than there was a soft booming sound that banked off the stone and marble walls. Each and every golden soldier stopped its approach. The ones nearest Abe swiveled about and looked Hellboy's way.

Nuada rose from the throne, his eyes bulging with disbelief.

"You challenge me?"

As one, nearly five thousand gold and red heads turned to face the king, who now stood on a ledge with his sister behind him.

"You bet your ass I do," Hellboy bellowed.

Abe had rushed between the frozen soldiers and was reunited with the others but he ignored them and came curiously close to Hellboy. He looked panic stricken and said, "No . . . please . . . no."

Focused solely on Nuada and not his friend, Hellboy nonchalantly said, "No choice, pal."

Hellboy walked away from his peers and toward the king, still standing in place, immobile like the army. Unlike them, though, his eyes were smoldering. Anger radiated from him like heat waves.

As he approached the king, the soldiers moved apart, allowing the challenger to pass unmolested.

He liked that.

Nearly reaching the elfin pair, Nuala stood beside her brother and said, "A challenge must be answered!" Her voice was projected so all could hear her.

"Who are you to challenge me?" Nuada questioned, sounding more like an insolent child than a ruler. "You're nobody! You are not royalty."

"Yes!" sister reminded brother. "He is Anung Un Rama—son of the Fallen One. He has the right!"

As king stared at the son of the Fallen One with newfound concern, Nuala gazed directly into Abe's eyes despite their distance. She was silently communicating to him that there was no other way to end this war before the army marched from Bethmoora to Earth. Once unleashed, there was little likelihood of stopping their carnage.

With a bitter smile, Nuada picked up his spear, a new piece fashioned atop the pole.

"Very well."

CHAPTER TWENTY-ONE

Nuada crouched low by the throne, grabbed a sword from its scabbard, and tossed it Hellboy's way.

Hellboy reached high to catch it and exposed his bare chest, which had started to ooze blood after the beating he had suffered at the hands of the army and that stone column. Grabbing the handle with one hand, he swished it back and forth, feeling more like Errol Flynn than anything else. He had loved to pretend sword fight back at the army base where he grew up. Broom was rarely indulgent and as a result, each duel was etched in his memory. As were the countless viewings of Flynn films but he needed to remember that this was no film, no script to follow. This was a fight to the death and truly, the fate of the world rested on the outcome.

No pressure.

Nuada spotted the fresh blood and commented with a sly smile, "You're bleeding. Most unfortunate."

Hellboy shrugged, wiping at his oozing chest wound with his free hand, not that it did him much good.

Both men waved their swords in the other's direction, acknowledging their readiness to begin. Then, like an uncaged leopard, Nuada sprang forward, teeth bared, eyes flashing and muscles rippling beneath his robes. Hellboy stood his ground, readying himself for the arrival.

His sword arm went up and the king's arm swung out.

The sound of steel against steel rang through the entire arena.

While not designed with acoustics in mind, the utter silence from the army allowed each and every noise to be heard clearly from end to end. Liz, Abe, and Krauss huddled together on one side, while Nuala remained safely by the throne. None would interfere and Nuada had no one to come to his aid. There would be no treachery, no Wink to help should things get tough.

Hellboy had done some work with a sword, but never considered himself proficient. He far preferred shooting things. Less mess, more distance. Nuada, though, had been practicing and fighting for countless years, so he was a master. Even feeling the flush of anger at being so challenged minutes after crowning himself king, his moves displayed an economy of motion.

Once his surprise rush was parried, he stood his ground, barely moving his feet as he ducked a heavy swing from Hellboy and then leapt high to avoid another. At least he wasn't playing with him, Hellboy considered. He wanted this over—and fast. That worked fine for him since it might mean the king would make a hasty move which he could exploit.

The swords clanged against one another again and again. Like dancers, they moved around the marble floor, close but not touching. Neither said a word but did his work, swinging, thrusting, parrying, and retreating. Hellboy could not recognize a style or pattern, nothing he could predict so he was constantly on the defensive. Part of his mind concentrated on forming an attack but it was constantly revised given their changing location.

Hellboy finally decided to try something he had read in an old pulp magazine. He growled, then roared and rushed forward in some form of berserker rage, swinging the sword in every direction, forcing the prince backward and managing to rip into the robes. It worked for a time, but he hadn't the strength to maintain such a rage and eventually, this would lead to a mistake that the king could exploit.

As they neared the B.P.R.D. agents, Abe cried out, "No . . . you cannot fight him—not without hurting her . . . "

He got it. The two were linked so any damage he did to the idiot king would also be done to the pretty princess. How on earth could he win such a battle?

Hellboy managed to drive Nuada to the center of the arena, gaining confidence since the king had not yet scored a blow. Both were slick with perspiration so Hellboy was definitely giving the king a workout. Of course, he had no idea what physiology was at work here and whether or not Nuada could tire before Hellboy did.

As they moved across the arena, nearly ten thousand artificial eyes watched with intent but no emotion. Their heads swiveled back and forth in perfect unison.

Nuada pressed an advantage and forced Hellboy atop one of the huge gears at one end of the marble walkway. In fact, Hellboy staggered and was pressed up against the giant gear until he rolled off, letting the king's blade bite steel, not meat.

Hellboy continued the retreat until they neared a wall and he turned his back on the king, rushed the wall, and sprang off it, flying clear over his enemy's head and landing in more open space.

With a growl, Nuada rushed after him and skidded on pebbles from the destruction of the stone columns. Hellboy had a clear shot and Abe caught his eye, silently pleading his case.

With his own low-throated growl, Hellboy avoided a killing blow, which in turn allowed Nuada to escape. They tracked one another back and forth around the arena. The silence was getting to Hellboy, preferring instead the roar of the crowd. After all, Nuada had home-field advantage and wasn't making much of it.

He had gotten careless, though, and, allowing Nuada to back him into one of those chunks of column, he stumbled. Nuada seized the opportunity and slashed at his chest, then his sword arm.

The silent spectators watched with calm intent.

Nuada thrust toward his heart but even wounded, Hellboy managed to get his sword up and parried the attack. He did so a second time and then a third but the arm was feeling heavy. This was not going to end well unless something changed.

The king thrust forward again, his eyes ablaze, but then, using his last supply of strength, Hellboy's hands grabbed on to the spear shaft. It was immobilized despite the extra effort the king expended.

It hurt to hold it in place. He was getting very weary and all he wanted to do was rest his eyes.

But, the world needed him to stop Nuada.

Liz needed him.

Their child needed him.

With a final effort, he ripped the spear from the king's hands and placed his sword at Nuada's throat.

Loud enough for all to hear, he said, "Enough."

King Nuada blinked at Hellboy. Surely, he had misheard what the offspring of the devil had said.

"No—you have to kill me," Nuada insisted. His eyes were angry and his voice taunted Hellboy. "I will not stop—I can't."

Tired and no longer possessing the energy or desire to fight, Hellboy repeated, "No. No more."

Lowering the sword and still possessing the spear, he looked deep into the king's eyes and declared, "I have won. You'll live."

Reaching out, causing the vanquished king to wince out of fear, Hellboy simply lifted the crown off his head. The king would live but be a prince once more.

Hellboy stood, dropping the spear out of Nuada's reach. Clutching the crown in his stone right hand and dragging the sword in his left, he walked back to Liz. Her welcoming, and relieved, smile was all he needed to begin feeling better.

Their moment was spoiled, of course, by the bellicose prince, who would not graciously accept his defeat. No, he rose to his own feet and challenged the man who had bested him.

"I will not bow to the humans. I will not," he declared. Such a spoiled brat.

With his usual smooth motion, he grabbed the lance from the floor and hefted it, his expression twisting to one of pure hatred.

He readied to hurl it into Hellboy's chest, a mortal blow if it connected.

All the army, still immobile, continued to observe the drama play out below their watchful eyes.

"Red!" Liz cried in warning.

The prince raised his spear, reared back and then stopped. Hellboy couldn't imagine what made him pause but then he understood. Blood blossomed on the front of his robes, spreading rapidly. He had been wounded, badly from the looks of it.

At first, his expression went quickly from anger to confusion to understanding. He turned slowly and saw Nuala standing nearby.

She had stabbed herself in the heart with a dagger. Her wound, staining her blue robes a deep purple, matched his exactly.

After Nuada acknowledged what had transpired, Nuala allowed herself to collapse and soon after, the prince followed.

He was gasping for breath but in a soft voice, in their Gaeilge tongue, he said, "Sister."

Her eyes fluttered and they stared at one another. Even from a distance, Hellboy could see that they were silently communing with one another. They had spent their lives inextricably intertwined, until recently, and they both loved and hated one another for their actions and choices.

Then they looked away from each other.

It was then that Abe broke free from the others and rushed to her side, unwilling to hold back his emotions. His love for her was clearly on display.

"No," he said softly, into her hair.

Carefully, he gathered the still-bleeding princess into his arms. She hung limply, still alive although barely.

"I never had a chance to tell you . . . how I felt. I never had the chance . . ." His voice drifted off, broken into a sob.

The princess smiled weakly at him, returning the affection.

"Give me your hand," she said, although it was soft and he had to strain to make out the words.

Without hesitation, he gave it to her and it rested between her two hands. They remained that way for several moments, neither saying a word. Then suddenly, she closed her eyes as tears began to flow freely. They were sad tears, each drop filled with regret.

"It is beautiful," she whispered.

"It's perfect," he agreed.

Hellboy wasn't sure what the hell they were talking about but it was too sad a moment to interrupt and display his ignorance. Instead, he wrapped a comforting arm around Liz, whose own eyes were damp as they witnessed what should have been a very private moment.

The princess then closed her eyes one final time and was at peace.

Knowing time was short, Hellboy walked from Liz to address the prince a last time. There'd be no tears shed on his behalf. He stopped in the center of the arena and studied the fallen prince. To his surprise, Nuada rose with a great effort and spoke first, as blood began to bubble up around his lips with each word.

"In the end, the humans . . . will tire of you. How much longer do you have? They've turned against you already . . . Them or us—which holocaust should be chosen?"

The humans had turned against him because of a chain reaction put into motion by Nuada himself. Hellboy had let his nature get away from him and used the circumstances to expose himself to the world, so he was a contributor to his own misery. Still, had the tooth fairies not struck, he would still have been chafing to expose himself. And had the elemental not been unleashed, he would not have contributed to the mass hysteria in Brooklyn. So, the dying prince was right; sooner or later, he'd be public knowledge and the contempt would eventually arrive.

"We die," the prince said in a halting voice. "And the world will be poorer for it."

With those final words, he fell to his knees and, as his father before him, turned from flesh to ash in a matter of seconds. He crumbled to the floor, a heap atop the gleaming marble.

Hellboy looked over at his friends and saw that the princess had not turned to ash and crumbled in Abe's arms, but instead had become a statue made from an alabaster stone.

Liz was openly crying, huddled by Krauss who stood by her.

Shaking his head at the circumstances, Hellboy looked back at the pile of ashes at his feet and stuck his left hand into the heap. He withdrew the crown which was coated in gray ash and glistened with far less luster than minutes ago.

He had won the battle, spared the prince's life, and could rightfully call himself the king of this land. All Bethmoora would acknowledge his sovereignty and should he choose to rule from here, he could ensure that man's world would be safe.

But this was not his world, nor were these his people. Their customs and traditions were alien to him. He could not rule them as wisely as Balor had lo these many centuries past.

Wearing the crown also gave him control of the Golden Army. By controlling it, he could also keep the world safe.

The options and possibilities inherent in the crescent crown were almost too much for Hellboy to contemplate.

"All that power . . . " he mused.

Rising to his feet, the crown still resting in his hand, he looked over at Johann and Liz. He couldn't look at Abe, not now.

He then looked around him at the patiently waiting soldiers, ready to accept their new master's orders.

Hellboy held out his left hand toward Liz, letting the crown dangle from his fingers.

She nodded and murmured to herself. There was a growing blue glow in the room and her right hand extended shooting forth a compact ball of fire.

The intensity of the heat he could handle despite gold being a good conductor. Slowly at first, then more rapidly, the crown began to soften, then melt. Huge gobs of molten gold dripped from his hand to splatter against the marble floor.

With each splash, row after row of golden soldier went dark. Row after row of coruscating red turned black and the army stood down.

Then the darkened soldiers fell down as no power controlled them, no crown directed their actions. The ones closest to the staircase tumbled down, creating a cacophony that echoed across the arena.

Liz was jubilant but her smile faded when she saw that Hellboy was troubled. Why wouldn't he be; after all, the prince's words had struck home.

He had given his time and nearly his life to protect the humans for years. Now they knew he existed, all of that was forgotten in favor of his devilish appearance and the fact that he dared love one of them.

"He's right," he told her. "The prince. How *do* we fit into this world?"

The last of the gold now cooling on the ground, he walked back to her and took her hand in his cooler, stone hand.

"Together. That's how," she assured him.

All thoughts of hearings and loss of political life were superseded by the notion that the people whom he would call friends were missing. Manning may have been a political creature, but he was not totally without feeling.

As a result, he tasked his section chiefs to book a private jet and get them to Ireland as soon as humanly possible. Now, twelve hours later, he was standing on the picturesque Giant's Causeway, under a bright blue sky, and could not imagine where his team had gone.

His concern for them had turned to impatience. The team he had brought along had studied every blade of grass and the nearest stone columns to seek any forensic evidence that the agents had been here. A lone raven watched them from a perch high above.

They had to be nearby, he knew, because the jet was parked in the distance. But there were no eyewitness reports, nothing to indicate where they were headed. Dr. Krauss had also taken the only copy of the map from the desk and he had rushed too fast to remember to have one made for himself. Not that he was any good with maps, but it was something.

"Nothing," he said, scanning the terrain once more. "Check for their belt locators," he ordered, even though they had been checked every fifteen minutes since their own plane had touched down. Nary a blip had been recorded.

Something changed in the air and Manning spun around, staring at the dark, ominous columns. Right before his eyes stood Krauss, Abe, Liz, and even Hellboy. Fortunately, only the latter seemed worse for wear and honestly, he could live with that. Less paperwork.

"Whoa! Where'd you come from?"

They gaped at him for a moment and Manning, focusing on Hellboy, realized it was all his fault. Everything from the moment the overgrown demon had crashed through the auction-house window. His lack of career growth was the red-skinned man's doing and he would hear about it.

Pointing right at Hellboy, he said, "You—you have a lot of explaining to do, young man."

Hellboy reached for a cigar, lit it up, and grinned sardonically at the government man.

"Hey, it's Manning, here to help. As always."

Approaching Manning, Hellboy removed his gun belt containing the Samaritan and draped it over Manning's outstretched arm.

"Wait a minute, wait a minute—what's going on?"

Hellboy, his back to Manning, was walking away slowly, clearly in pain. Liz was nearby, smiling at him. That was odd—weren't they on the outs? He suddenly realized the depth of how much he did not know and that it was clearly going to come back and bite him in the ass.

"I quit," Hellboy told Manning.

"Are you serious?"

Manning just stared, eyes wide, jaw dropped. It must have appeared comical to the others but he had no clue whether or not to be happy about this or worried.

Liz neared him and answered for the ex-agent.

"Looks that way, doesn't it?"

With that, she and Abe walked past him and after Hellboy who had yet to slow down.

"What's wrong with you?" he demanded out loud. "You can't all quit."

From the growing distance, Hellboy answered, "Watch us."

Hellboy started to leave the parkland but hesitated. Was he finally coming to his senses?

"On second thought," he said, and walked back toward Manning. Okay, they could work this out, he considered. It would take every last connection he still had in Washington, but he could salvage this mess. He was *that* good.

Manning smiled encouragingly at Hellboy but the smile was not returned. All Hellboy did was reach out and grab the Samaritan.

"I think I'll keep this."

With that, he returned to Liz and Abe, and the three strolled off together.

Something had happened and something was happening. It was all unraveling again and that could not be condoned. He turned to Krauss who had stood by, watching in silence. Without a face, Manning had no clue what was going on in his mind.

"They can't do this. Stop them, Johann."

He glared in the direction of the departing agents, their fellow agents giving them a wide berth.

Krauss walked over to Manning and said, "Manning, you're a jerk."

Hellboy and Liz walked ahead of Abe and they watched as Dr. Krauss walked away from Manning to join them. That was certainly unexpected—but given the last few hours, maybe not.

Away from the stone gateway, and the other agents, they could hear a breeze in the air. The air was warm and things felt right with the world.

There were still things that needed tending to, starting with healing his chest wound, and the matter of cleaning out his quarters before someone pilfered his audio collection. He, no, *they* would need a place to live, big enough for them and the cats . . . and the baby.

Now that they had saved the world again, it was time to talk about that.

Liz interlaced her fingers in his and they walked another few feet in silence before either spoke.

"What you said before—about us living anywhere . . ." she began in a soft voice.

"Anywhere!" he proclaimed. "You and me, let's find a place in the country. Clean air, green hills . . ."

He drifted off, peering across the vast greenery and images danced in his mind.

"A yard! With lots of room to grow in. It'll be great for the baby."

Hellboy looked at Liz expectantly, hoping she too wanted the all-American dream.

"Babies."

He took a few additional steps and then stopped dead in his tracks. Spinning about, he gaped at Liz, who continued to smile. She was beautiful when she smiled. It was true—women glowed when they were pregnant and she didn't need her internal flame to do that. Not now.

"Babies?"

Liz raised two fingers, grinning even more broadly.

"Two."

His grin threatened to eclipse her own.

EPILOGUE

The cold, forbidding wind did not deter the five helicopters from approaching the appropriate glacier. They were identical, dark choppers, each flashing the logo for Zinco Enterprises, a global concern.

Nicknamed Amundsen's Glacier, it was named after Roald Amundsen, a Norwegian explorer who had led the first expedition to the South Pole a century previous. Where it was once six miles wide and some one hundred and twenty-eight miles long, global warming in the recent past had reduced the glacier to two-thirds that dimension. Intriguingly, it was not named by Amundsen himself, but by Laurence Gould, the man who had actually first approached the glacier after Admiral Byrd spotted it from the air.

As the choppers touched down on the hard, icy surface, which drained from the south and west of the Nilsen Plateau, a set of thickly covered guards appeared out of nowhere and surrounded the vehicles as they powered down.

Once the blades slowed to safe speed, one of the doors slid open and from it emerged a man carrying a metallic box big enough to store a good-sized cowboy hat. He was perfectly groomed, not at all caring about the bitter chill in the air.

With practiced ease, he walked toward a crevice, the same one the heavily armed guards had exited from. He walked down the slope and some distance, enjoying the solitude that the glacier provided him.

Such a large, inhospitable, and difficult-to-access location was the perfect hiding place for Zinco's private work. He had seen to it the space below was self-contained and self-sufficient, so much so, that it had not needed resupplying for years.

After several minutes of walking, the stony corridor led him to an underground laboratory that had been built in this space decades earlier. While relatively clean, the equipment was incredibly outdated with boxy machines sporting cathode ray tubes and Tesler coils. A faint odor of ozone could be detected, caused by burned-out wiring from years before. Wires and cords stretched along the floor and some were tacked into the walls. None obscured the large, red-and-white flag with the black swastika in the center.

Beyond the ancient, but still functional equipment that had been state of the art more than five decades previous, were huge alcoves containing weapons that were the product of madmen's dreams. Small and large firearms were placed on racks, alongside devices designed to emit radiation or electronic death. Trucks, to carry men and material, stood beside tanks that packed more firepower than any panzer.

Beyond them, in a separate space, stood an eight-foot-tall robot, its joints and gears on display. The body remained highly polished, well cared for through the years. All it lacked was a head.

The man, billionaire Roderick Zinco, was carrying that very object in his hands.

Zinco had lived a long, prosperous life, thanks to his association with the mystics who had served the Third Reich over sixty years ago. Since then, he had funneled his vast

resources into the collection and study of the occult, a yin to
Bruttenholm's yang. While amassing countless billions, he
remained focused on serving his masters, seeing to it their hopes,
dreams, and plans would be obeyed and brought to fruition.

That was all coming true today.

He approached the robot reverently. His eyes gleaming
with anticipation and more than a little madness, he reached
up and managed to affix the box-thing to the body. Rapidly,
his hands flew around the juncture, snapping the head into
place, making certain every fit was just right.

Before he could finish, pistons began to pump and the
fastening became automated with loud snaps and pops. Then
the four side panels rose simultaneously, revealing the true
head, that of Karl Ruprect Kroenen.

It remained encased in the tight-fitting mask that did
double-duty: hiding his hideously scared face and filtering
out the germs that Kroenen feared above all else. The masked
head floated in a thick, green liquid held in place within a
glass jar. The severed neck ended with exposed wires that
connected to the base of the jar and then slithered through
prepared openings to connect to the main body.

Once the connections were complete, the body rumbled
once and the left leg moved forward. The right followed and
the resurrected robot strode forward several feet, Zinco clapping his hands in delight. This was better than Christmas
morning for the industrialist.

Best of all, Kroenen smiled at the movement, the freedom
and the new life promised by this new form. He'd been alive
since 1897, in one form or another; now the only organic
matter left to him was his brain and in the end, that was all
that truly mattered.

When he was last conscious, it was to see a giant cog
dropped on him by Hellboy. The red-skinned demon and his

keeper, Bruttenholm, had been dogging his trail for decades, complicating his goals and destroying his body bit by bit, beginning with the loss of his left hand the day Hellboy came to Earth.

"It's all exactly as you promised," Zinco said.

From behind him, hidden in the dark shadows of the glacier, emerged a black robed form. He carried a leather book in his hand and steam escaped from the gaping hole in his chest.

Grigori Yefimovich Rasputin stepped beside Zinco, watching the reborn Kroenen flex his new arms and legs. He nodded with approval and said, "And so shall be the end of it all."

THE END

ACKNOWLEDGMENTS

No book is written in a vacuum and a novelization especially owes its existence to numerous people beyond its author.

First, I've known Mike Mignola for over twenty years and have enjoyed his storytelling during that span of time. Watching him grow into a master of the medium has been a delight and his willingness to chat about the movie and help flesh out the screenplay was a delight.

Guillermo del Toro was the champion who brought this comic book character to life and sustained it in the public consciousness. His affection for Mike's world is evident on every page of the screenplay which was easy to adapt.

At Universal, thanks to Daniel McPeek for all his help and support.

At Dark Horse, I have to single out their unsung hero, editor Rob Simpson. We've known each other well over twenty-five years and our ability to work together has been very infrequent so when he called to offer this project, it was a great thrill. His care and attention to detail has been terrific, making for a better reading experience.

At home, no project can get done without the love and support of my wife Deb, who nods sympathetically as I regale her with the day's travails. Robbie popped in and out of the office wondering when we'd get to see the finished film and Dixie the wonder dog continued to sit at my feet as the screenplay became novel.

ROBERT GREENBERGER is a nearly thirty-year veteran of working in the world of pop culture. A graduate of Binghamton University, he began his career at Starlog Press as managing editor of *Fangoria* and created *Comics Scene*—the first nationally distributed magazine to cover comic books, comic strips, and animation. In 1984, he joined DC Comics where he enjoyed a sixteen-year career in Editorial and Editorial Administration. After a ten-month detour onto the information superhighway at Gist Communications, he was lured back to comic books. Spending 2001 at Marvel Comics as its Director–Publishing Operations proved exhausting and enlightening. He returned to DC Comics for four years as a Senior Editor in its collected-editions department where he helped inaugurate new formats. Bob then joined the staff of *Weekly World News* where he was its managing editor until the paper unceremoniously folded in 2007.

As a freelance writer, Bob has written over a dozen young adult nonfiction titles, from a biography of Will Eisner to the History of Pakistan. He has also written many *Star Trek* novels and short stories, both on his own and in collaboration with others. Bob has also written a smattering of original science fiction and fantasy. Previously for DH Books, he cowrote *Predator: Flesh & Blood* with Michael Jan Friedman. In 2008, he also wrote DelRey Books' *Essential Batman Encyclopedia*.

He lives in Connecticut where he serves as Moderator for Fairfield's Representative Town Meeting. He makes his home with his wife Deb and son Robbie. His daughter Kate grew up and suddenly became an adult, currently living in Maryland.

HELLBOY ™ by MIKE MIGNOLA